ENTREPRENEURSHIP
SIMPLIFIED, AMPLIFIED, & VISUALIZED

By Clay Clark

2

ISBN: 978-1-7364217-4-1

Entrepreneurship Simplified, Amplified and Visualized.
Copyright © 2020 by Clay Clark Publishing
Published by Clay Clark Publishing
3920 W 91st Street South
Tulsa, OK 74132

3

By default, 96% of businesses fail.
INC. MAGAZINE
https://www.inc.com/bill-carmody/why-96-of-businesses-fail-within-10-years.html

STOP THROWING GUTTER BALLS!

① ESTABLISH REVENUE GOALS [$]

What are your yearly gross revenue goals? _____

What are your total weekly gross revenue goals? _____

② DETERMINE THE BREAK-EVEN NUMBERS

Number of customers / sales to break even? _____

③ DEFINE WORK WEEK: NUMBER OF HOURS

How many hours are you willing to work? _____

What are your boundaries? _____

⑥ CREATE 3-LEGGED MARKETING STOOL

Leg 1 _____

Leg 2 _____

Leg 3 _____

⑤ IMPROVE BRANDING

On a scale of 1-10, with 10 being the highest, how highly would you rate your website, print pieces, and social media? _____

④ DEFINE YOUR UNIQUE VALUE PROPOSITION:

Who are your top 3 competitors? _____

Have you mystery shopped your competitors? _____

⑦ CREATE A SALES CONVERSION SYSTEM $

Sales scripts? _____

Recorded calls? _____

One sheets? _____

Pre-Written emails? _____

Lead trackers? _____

⑧ DETERMINE SUSTAINABLE CUSTOMER ACQUISITION COSTS

What does it cost to Obtain each customer? _____

Do you have a tracking Sheet? _____

Weekly advertising spend? _____

⑨ CREATE REPEATABLE SYSTEMS, PROCESSES, AND FILE ORGANIZATION

What daily, core, repeatable, actionable processes are not documented into script or checklist form? _____

What processes and Systems are not repeatable? _____

Do you have checklists for all positions?

4

CREATE A SALES CONVERSION SYSTEM (7)

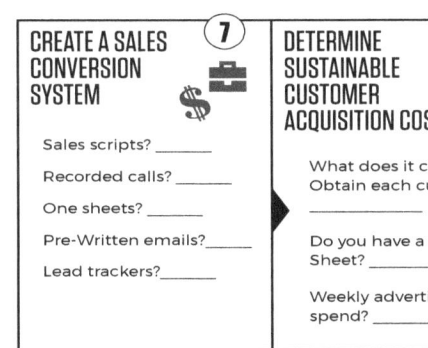

Sales scripts? _____

Recorded calls? _____

One sheets? _____

Pre-Written emails? _____

Lead trackers? _____

DETERMINE SUSTAINABLE CUSTOMER ACQUISITION COSTS (8)

What does it cost to Obtain each customer?

_____

Do you have a tracking Sheet? _____

Weekly advertising spend? _____

CREATE REPEATABLE SYSTEMS, PROCESSES, AND FILE ORGANIZATION (9)

What daily, core, repeatable, actionable processes are not documented into script or checklist form?_____

What processes and Systems are not repeatable? _____

Do you have checklists for all positions?

5

CREATE HUMAN RESOURCES AND RECRUITMENT SYSTEMS (12)

- Who are your A players? _____
- Who are your B players? _____
- Who are your C players? _____
- When is your weekly staff meeting? _____
- When is your weekly group interview? _____

CREATE A SUSTAINABLE AND REPETITIVE WEEKLY SCHEDULE (11)

When is your weekly group interview?_____

When is your daily group huddle?_____

CREATE MANAGEMENT EXECUTION SYSTEMS (10)

What people on your team will not do their jobs?

_____

Do you have merit-based pay installed? _____

CREATE YOUR ACCOUNTING AND AUTOMATE THE EARNING OF MILLIONS (13)

Are you using Clay Clark's Ultimate Tracking Sheet?_____

DETERMINE THE POINT OF ACHIEVING FINANCIAL SUCCESS?

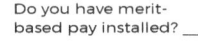

F7 GOALS (14)

1·Faith _____
2·Family _____
3·Friendship _____
4·Fitness _____
5·Finances _____
6·Fun _____
7·Focus _____

"NOTABLE QUOTABLES"

"If you can't explain it simply, you don't understand it well enough."

- Albert Einstein

(The man whose vast knowledge allowed us to create the Manhattan Project and the weapons needed to defeat the hate-mongering-satan-inspired-pro-genocide Axis powers which included Nazi Germany, Italy, Japan and that ass-clown and manipulative fascist leader Adolf Hitler. May he burn in hell.)

DEDICATION

This book is dedicated to my kids Havana, Aubrey Napoleon-Hill, Angelina, Laya, and Scarlett. I hope this book is explained so simply that it demonstrates that I (your Dad), actually knows what I am talking about. Having you 5 and your mom has given me 6 more reasons to keep on going. Making money has always been easy for me, it's the rest of life that has been hard for me. May the ceiling of my success be the floor of your success.

"NOTABLE QUOTABLES"

"Education is what remains after one has forgotten what one has learned in school."

- Albert Einstein
  (The man whose vast knowledge allowed us to create the Manhattan Project and the weapons needed to defeat the pro-genocide Axis powers which includes Nazi Germany, Italy and Japan.)

INTRODUCTION

Throughout my career I have been blessed to achieve tremendous success both as an entrepreneur and as a podcast host. However, I have not forgotten where I have come from and I always have had a burning desire to teach people the proven moves that they can implement and use to also start and grow a time freedom and financial freedom creating business. However, as I was rereading the Albert Einstein quote, "If you can't explain it simply, you don't understand it well enough," I thought to myself that Albert was challenging me from the grave and pushing me to write a book that would break-down and explain how entrepreneurship works in a way that everybody can understand. And thus, you now hold in your hand, the book, *Entrepreneurship Simplified, Amplified and Visualized*. I hope and pray that this book will expose you to the world of entrepreneurship in a very approachable and coachable way so that both YOU and YOUR family can experience what it is like to enjoy both time and financial freedom.

TABLE OF CONTENTS

CHAPTER 1
What is Entrepreneurship? Why Most People Are Going the Wrong Way, but They Will Passionately Tell You That Your Gas Cap is Open.

CHAPTER 2
Don't Reinvent the Wheel. Earning Time and Financial Freedom is Not Complicated or "Woo, Woo." You Just Have to Master the Following Skills to Earn More Than Enough to Pay Your Bills.

CHAPTER 3
Escaping the Wage Cage Requires Paranoia and Passion. Entrepreneurship is Not for Most People.

CHAPTER 4
If You Hit Snooze, You Lose as An Entrepreneur.

CHAPTER 5
Focus On What You Can Control and Don't Watch the Weather Channel When Possible.

CHAPTER 6
Without the Ability to Sell, Your Business Dreams Will Go to Hell.

CHAPTER 7
Once You Nail It, You Must Scale It or to the Idea of Time Freedom You Must Say to Hell With It!

CHAPTER 8
You Must Commit to Your Business Because Nobody Else is Going to Care About Your Business As Much As You.

CHAPTER 9
Most People Die at the Age of 25, But Are Not Buried Until the Age of 75.

CHAPTER 10
Time is Your Most Precious Asset. You Can Always Make More Money, But You Can't Make More Time.

CHAPTER 11
It's All About Resourcefulness and Not About Resources. Start Now with What You Have. The Time Will Never Be Just Right.

CHAPTER 12
Don't Ask Most People for Advice and Don't Listen to Their Unsolicited Advice.

CHAPTER 13
Measure What You Treasure, Track Reality and Don't Run Your Business Based Upon Projections.

CHAPTER 14
Stop Guessing, Hoping, Wishing, and Praying for Directions. Use MAPs, GPS, and Guides That Have Clearly Demonstrated That They Know the Proven Path.

CHAPTER 15
Recognize That Action is the Real Measure of Intelligence.

CHAPTER 16
Marketing is Simply a Contest for Getting the Attention of Your Ideal and Likely Buyers.

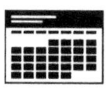

CHAPTER 17
Design Your Schedule and Design Your Life or Someone Else Will.

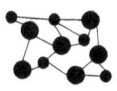

CHAPTER 18
Your Network is Your Net Worth - Stop Hanging Around Negative, Soul-Sucking, Excuse-Making, and Leeching Family, Friends, Employees, and Business People.

CHAPTER 19
You Must Learn to Lead People, to Fire Idiots, and to Become an Enemy of Average or You Will Lose.

CHAPTER 20
Schedule Time for What Matters Most and Live Intentionally.

CHAPTER 1

What is Entrepreneurship? Why Most People Are
Going the Wrong Way, but They Will Passionately
Tell You That Your Gas Cap is Open.

19

What does it mean to be an entrepreneur? An entrepreneur is simply a human who solves a problem for other humans in exchange for a profit. Don't over-spiritualize this. Just think about problems that you can solve for people that they are actually willing to pay to have solved.

1.

People don't want to mow their lawns or to maintain the vegetation that is located around the exterior of their homes, thus landscaping is an industry.

"EVERYONE HERE HAS THE SENSE THAT RIGHT
NOW IS ONE OF THOSE MOMENTS WHEN WE ARE
INFLUENCING THE FUTURE."
–STEVE JOBS
CO-FOUNDER, CHAIRMAN, AND CEO OF APPLE

2.

While working out of his parent's garage, Steve Jobs realized that the average human would never use a computer that required complex code. Thus he worked with his partner, Steve Wozniak, to create personal computers that the average non-nerd could use in route to creating the world's most valuable company, which is now known as Apple.

3.

Henry Ford recognized that owning, feeding, and loving on a horse was not a very efficient way to get from point A to point B. However, he also recognized that most humans, in America, at the time were not SUPER RICH. Thus, he created the Model T automobile which made it affordable for the average American to own an automobile, and he earned millions as a result of it.

"ALL THE SMILES IN THE WORLD AREN'T GOING
TO HELP YOU IF YOUR PRODUCT OR SERVICE IS
NOT WHAT THE CUSTOMER WANTS."

"THE SERVICE PROFIT CHAIN"

4.

I realized years ago that men want to have their haircut in a place that feels like a country club or a man cave. I realized that men wanted to actually enjoy their grooming experience as opposed to having to endure it. Thus, I created, financed, branded, marketed, and successfully staffed the creation of The Elephant In The Room Men's Grooming Lounge - www.EITRLounge.com.

5.

I realized at the age of 15, that the average disc jockey was disorganized, and disinterested in their audience, thus I started "C & G DJ Service" which went on to become "DJConnection.com." The reason I was able to grow it into the nation's largest wedding entertainment service is because I saw the problem that most DJs were terrible and I solved it by systematically taking events and weddings from ordinary to extraordinary.

YOUR BUSINESS EXISTS TO SOLVE PROBLEMS
FOR YOU AND YOUR CUSTOMERS.
- CLAY CLARK
FOUNDER OF THRIVE

Action Steps

Make a list of the problems that you can solve for other humans on the planet that people are actually willing to pay to have solved:

Problem That You Can Solve #1: _____

Problem That You Can Solve #2: _____

Problem That You Can Solve #3: _____

Problem That You Can Solve #4: _____

Problem That You Can Solve #5: _____

Problem That You Can Solve #6: _____

Problem That You Can Solve #7: _____

Problem That You Can Solve #8: _____

Problem That You Can Solve #9: _____

Problem That You Can Solve #10: _____

"ENTREPRENEURS SOLVE THE WORLD'S PROBLEMS AND UNAPOLOGETICALLY MAKE MONEY DOING IT."
   - CLAY CLARK

Don't over complicate the path to creating a business that will allow you to earn both time and financial freedom. You must avoid the advice from most people when it comes to starting a business. YOU MUST REMEMBER that most people are wrong about most things most of the time, so don't ask MOST people for advice about MOST things. You must realize that we live in a weird world where *Forbes* now reports that 70% of people hate their jobs, where *Inc. Magazine* shares that 85% of potential employees lie on their resumes, where *Inc. Magazine* reports that 96% of businesses fail within 10 years, where 47% of Americans leach from the system and pay no taxes, where the *Washington Post* reports that 78% of men have cheated on their spouse, and where *CNN Money* reports that 40% of Americans now have less than $400 saved. A big problem is that most people are passionate about the wrong things.

They are passionate about how popular they are, how many Instagram followers they have, and whether your gas tank is open while you drive down the road. I have literally had people passionately yell at me that I am driving down the road with an open gas tank, but I have never had a SUPER SUCCESSFUL PERSON pull me aside and tell me that I am going in the wrong direction with my life. Do not listen to most people about most things, most of the time. Listen to people who are in shape when it comes to fitness, and listen to people who are financially successful when it comes to finances. Don't listen to most people most of the time, because most people are wrong about most things most of the time. Find the people who actually have the answers you need, and ask them. You are fortunate to be going through this book because I have the answers when it comes to building a successful business.

FUN! FACTS!

→ 70% of your employees hate their jobs.
- Forbes
*https://www.forbes.com/sites/
carminegallo/2011/11/11/your-emotionally-
disconnected-employees/*

→ 85% of Job Applicants Lie on Resumes.
- Inc.
*https://www.inc.com/jt-odonnell/staggering-
85-of-job-applicants-lying-on-resumes-.html*

→ 96% of Businesses Fail Within 10 Years.
- Inc.
*https://www.inc.com/bill-carmody/why-96-of-
businesses-fail-within-10-years.html*

More than 44% of Americans pay no federal income tax.
- Market Watch
https://www.marketwatch.com/story/81-million-americans-wont-pay-any-federal-income-taxes-this-year-heres-why-2018-04-16

 40% of Americans can't cover a $400 emergency expense.
- CNN Money
https://www.washingtonpost.com/opinions/five-myths-about-cheating/2012/02/08/glQANGdaBR_story.html?noredirect=on

NOTABLE QUOTABLE:

"If you cannot save money, the seeds of greatness are not in you."

- W. Clement Stone
(The founder of the Combined Insurance Company of America which once had over $1 Billion in assets.)

"NOTABLE QUOTABLES"

"Opinions are the cheapest commodities on earth. Everyone has a flock of opinions ready to be wished upon anyone who will accept them. If you are influenced by "opinions" when you reach DECISIONS, you will not succeed in any undertaking."

- Napoleon Hill
(The best-selling self-help author of all-time and the personal apprentice of Andrew Carnegie who was once the world's wealthiest man despite having grown up impossibly poor.)

FUN FACTS!

During the process of writing the book *Everyday Millionaires,* written by the Dave Ramsey disciple and best-selling author Chris Hogan, Chris and his team conducted the largest study EVER on the mindsets of millionaires. During their research they surveyed over 10,000 U.S. millionaires and they discovered that:

➡️ 75% of millennials and 52% of baby boomers believe that millionaires inherited their wealth. These beliefs are wrong.

➡️ In fact, according to the massive research project, *"A 2017 survey from Fidelity Investments found that 88 percent of millionaires are self-made."*

CHAPTER 2

Don't Reinvent the Wheel. Earning Time and
Financial Freedom is Not Complicated or "Woo,
Woo." You Just Have to Master the Following Skills
to Earn More Than Enough to Pay Your Bills.

THE WHEEL OF WEALTH
DON'T REINVENT THE WHEEL

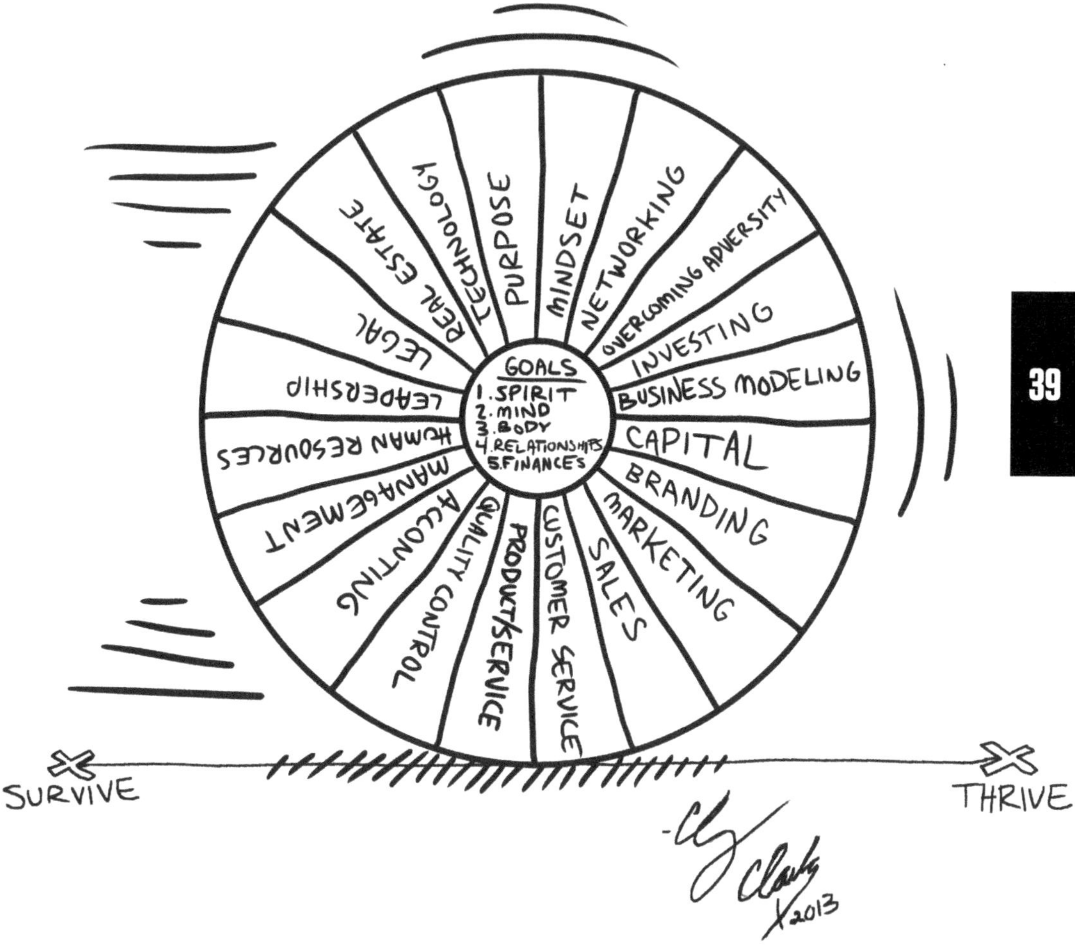

GOALS
1. SPIRIT
2. MIND
3. BODY
4. RELATIONSHIPS
5. FINANCES

PURPOSE
MINDSET
NETWORKING
OVERCOMING ADVERSITY
INVESTING
BUSINESS MODELING
CAPITAL
BRANDING
MARKETING
SALES
CUSTOMER SERVICE
PRODUCT/SERVICE
QUALITY CONTROL
ACCOUNTING
MANAGEMENT
HUMAN RESOURCES
LEADERSHIP
LEGAL
REAL ESTATE
TECHNOLOGY

SURVIVE

THRIVE

39

Clark
X2013

In order to create a business that will produce both time and financial freedom for you and your future family, you don't have to reinvent the wheel. In fact, earning both time and financial freedom is not complicated, "woo, woo," or the result of luck. If you live in America during the time that I am writing this book, in order to become financially "successful," all you have to do is to master the skills in the drawing on the next page.

In the world of entrepreneurship you don't earn additional income as a result of being the most original person on the planet. In fact, you often get penalized for trying to be the most creative person. If you want to succeed in the world of entrepreneurship, it is better to be a pirate than a pioneer.

It's better to stand on the shoulders of the giants to get a better look. It's better to invest the time needed to see what your biggest competitor is doing so that you can "one-up" them.

The Road Map

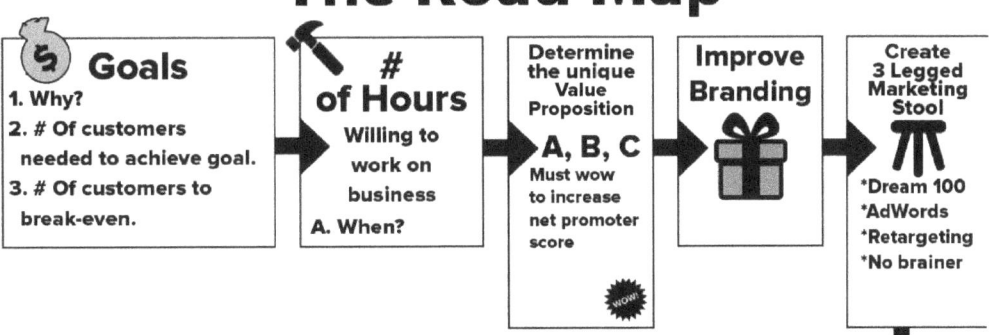

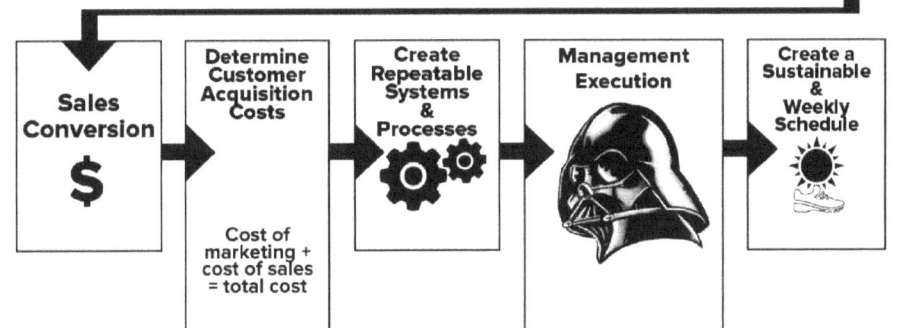

F6 Goals

1. Faith
2. Family
3. Friendship

4. Fitness
5. Family
6. Fun

I worry that you won't like entrepreneurship if you look at it from the wrong perspective. My goals are my goals and your goals are your goals, but at the end of the day, a business exists to create both time and financial freedom for the owner of the business. You must invest the time needed to determine how many customers you must add value to in exchange for the annual income that you are seeking. As an example, if you are a real estate agent and you make an average of $6,000 per deal, how many deals do you need per year to achieve your financial goals?

"IF I HAVE SEEN FARTHER, IT IS BECAUSE I HAVE BEEN ABLE TO STAND ON THE SHOULDERS OF GIANTS."
- SIR ISAAC NEWTON
ENGLISH PHYSICIST AND MATHMETICIAN

43

Action Items

You must invest the time RIGHT NOW to determine how much money you need to earn on an annual basis in order to earn enough money to fund the achievement of the goals that you have set for yourself and your family in the areas of:

1. What are your faith goals for this year? _____

2. When are you going to pursue these goals every week? _____

3. How much money will it cost you to pursue these goals each week? _____

4. What are your family goals for this year? _____

5. When are you going to pursue these goals every week? _____

6. How much money will it cost you to pursue these goals each week? _____

7. What are your financial goals for this year? _____

8. When are you going to pursue these goals every week? _____

9. How much money will it cost you to pursue these goals each week? _____

10. What are your fitness goals for this year? _____

11. When are you going to pursue these goals every week? _____

12. How much money will it cost you to pursue these goals each week? _____

13. What are your friendship goals for this year? _____

14. When are you going to pursue these goals every week? _____

15. How much money will it cost you to pursue these goals each week? _____

16. What are your fun goals for this year? _____

17. When are you going to pursue these goals every week? _____

18. How much money will it cost you to pursue these goals each week? _____

Don't think that you have to share my goals in order to become a successful entrepreneur. I like to work because work is what I like to do. I like firing people that are not a good fit for our office culture. I can't stand to be around lazy people and people that don't appreciate working hard and playing hard. The office culture I like has the intensity of the *Braveheart* movie with the comedic relief of a predictable Adam Sandler film. I don't like going out to eat

"I have nothing in common with lazy people who blame others for their lack of success. Great things come from hard work and perseverance. No Excuses."

— Kobe Bryant
(An 18 time NBA All-star and the 2008 NBA most valuable player.)

because I find it to be expensive, inefficient, and a place to run into people that I have fired during my 23 years of being self-employed. However, you don't have to think like me in every area to become a successful entrepreneur. A business exists to serve you. As for me, my business exists to allow me to write books like this in my man-cave while burning pinion wood and repetitively listening to the *Beautiful Mind* soundtrack. This is the life I want so this is what I choose to do with my time and financial freedom.

– – – – – – – – – – – – – – – – – –

"I work but it's not work. I love what I do so it's no longer work. Work for me is like going on a two week vacation."

– President Donald Trump

I don't like vacations because I really enjoy my daily life. I view vacation as a distraction from the traction I'm gaining as I gradually and methodically, day by day, turn my goals, dreams, and visions into reality. However, if you want to vacation constantly, that does not make you wrong, a bad person, or someone that does not qualify to become a successful entrepreneur. I am not writing this to tell you what your goals should be. I am writing this to teach you the specific moves that you can use to create a business that will allow you to earn enough income to afford to live a life that you will love.

FUN FACT:

70% of your employees hate their jobs
- Forbes

https://www.forbes.com/sites/ carminegallo/2011/11/11/your-emotionally-disconnected-employees/

I detest, dislike, and loathe the thought of going on vacation. The best-selling author, entrepreneur and founder of Yoyodyne, which was sold to Yahoo for $30,000,000, Seth Godin, was correct when he once wrote, "Instead of wondering when your next vacation is, maybe you should set up a life you don't need to escape from."

"NOTABLE QUOTABLES"

"The goal is to be able to live your life the way Michael Jordan played basketball, or Marvin Gaye sang a song. To be able to feel the way you feel when you laugh at a joke, but to feel that way all the time."

- Russell Simmons
(The co-founder of Def Jam Recordings, the co-producer of the hit film, The Nutty Professor, the founder of the clothing lines, Phat Farm, Argyleculture, and Tantris who is worth approximately $340 million. Russell Simmons is the promoter, and record executive responsible for introducing the world to LL Cool J, Run DMC, the Beastie Boys, and other early hip hop pioneers.)

When I'm at "the office," I love the music that is played overhead (because I chose it). I love what I eat (because I chose it). I love the people that work at the office (because I chose them and they chose our company). I love the clients that I work with (because I chose them and they chose me). I love the smell of burning pinion wood which I burn at the office. I love to arrive at work at 4:00 AM (because there is no rush hour traffic at 4:00 AM). I love to leave the office at 2:30 PM (because there is no rush hour traffic at 2:30 PM). I really just love every aspect of every day. However, the rest of life doesn't make sense to me, and so that is not what this book is about.

96% of businesses fail within 10 years.
- Inc. Magazine

https://www.inc.com/bill-carmody/why-96-of-businesses-fail-within-10-years.html

I don't understand why family members that I have financially invested in would steal money from me. I don't understand why friends, family, and business partners would choose to have sex with people they are not married to. I don't know why Christians would fight over petty things to the point that the world now has (according to Quora.com) 34,000 different denominations. I don't understand why people want to argue about religion and politics. However, I do understand how to build a successful, scalable, time & financial freedom-creating business. That is what this book is about.

FUN FACT:

In 2019, my average client grew by 104%.

*Visit **Thrivetimeshow.com/does-it-work** to see their results.*

CHAPTER 3

Escaping the Wage Cage Requires Paranoia and
Passion. Entrepreneurship is Not for Most People.

LEAVE THE CAGE.
AVOID THE VIKING.
GET THE MONEY.

Note:
The Viking wants to kill you as soon as
you chase your bags of money and that
Viking represents competition, doubts, fear,
adversity, and perpetual rejection.

If you interview the average person, they will tell you that they want to be successful, or that they want to own their own business, but entrepreneurship is simply not for everybody. In order to be successful as an entrepreneur, you must accept the fact that you have to successfully escape "the wage cage" and enter into a reality where you are free to chase bags of money (success). You also must realize that you are now living in a world where Vikings (your competitors) are willing to do anything they can in order to take what you have worked so hard for. In the world of entrepreneurship, the competition is fierce and only the paranoid survive. On planet Earth, strength is only gained through struggle. In order to escape from the norm and to live a life filled with massive success, you must embrace that you will also live a life filled with endless adversity. Just this week, Seth Godin let us know that we cannot include the transcript of our interview with him in an upcoming book that I am working on, *Mastermind Manuscripts*. The hit-writing song-writer Ross Golan rejected me for the book too. However, the legendary best-selling leadership author and speaker John Maxwell said that I could include the transcript of my interview with him in my upcoming book.

"The way to get started is to quit talking and begin doing. It's kind of fun to do the impossible. All our dreams can come true, if we have the courage to pursue them."

- Walt Disney
(The co-founder of the Disney empire)

The late Clayton Christensen, the *New York Times* best-selling author who served as the Kim B. Clark Professor of Business Administration at the Harvard Business School, also said before his death in 2019 that we could use his interview. As an entrepreneur, your day will be filled with both incredible wins and soul-sucking and dream-killing rejections and losses. The world of entrepreneurship is the world I love.

At this point, I have lost track of how many times our top employees have gone on to become our top competitors, (until I crushed them). At this point, I have lost track of how many employees have stolen tangible goods, intellectual property, and top-performing employees. I can also tell you that it no longer bothers me when these terrible things happen. I expect them and I embrace them as part of the game, just as a football player expects injuries and chronic pain to be part of their job description.

I've learned to accept that in order to create the EPIC life that I have always wanted, and that I now live, I must embrace that epic stories always involve a character who must overcome major adversity in route to achieving their ultimate success. This is what I have had to do as an entrepreneur on a daily basis since the age of just 16 years old. If you are prepared to embrace the wins and rejections of the entrepreneurial life then sign and date below before you continue reading!

Name_____   Date:_____

"Blessed are those who are persecuted for their righteousness (being correct and honest), for theirs is the kingdom of heaven."

- Matthew 5:10

(Saint Matthew was put to death based upon the orders of the King of Ethiopia while celebrating mass. The King lusted after his own niece, who was a nun and thus he was rebuked by Matthew.)

"WHERE THERE IS NO VISION, THE PEOPLE PERISH."

- PROVERBS 29:18

WE ARE ALMOST TO THE PROMISED LAND, GUYS! JUST RIGHT OVER THIS HILL.

CHAPTER 4

"Every day, you must rise and grind. When you hit snooze, you lose."

- Clay Clark
    (The founder DJ Connection, EITRLounge.com, EpicPhotos.com, MakeYourLifeEpic.com, etc.)

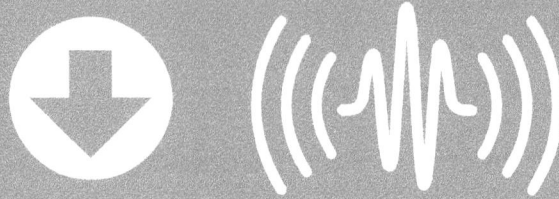

"I only go to sleep so that I can do it again."

— Bishop T.D. Jakes
(The pastor of the Potter's House mega church, the New York Times best-selling author and award-winning film maker)

"When you're around enormously successful people you realize their success isn't an accident. It's about work."

- Ryan Tedder

 (The Grammy award-winning singer and song writer who actually sang at our wedding and who has written hit songs for U2, Beyonce, Taylor Swift, Kelly Clarkson, and countless huge artists.)

"NOTABLE QUOTABLES"

"I'm discovering that the people that wake up early are really the trendsetters. They are up giving the commands on what the whole world needs to do, so the worker wakes up at 8am but the dreamer, the innovator, the creator, the engineer is up at 3 or 4 in the morning making it happen."

- Eric Thomas
(The Thrivetime Show guest and the legendary motivational speaker)

"The latest I will get up is 6:30 AM. Sometimes I will get to the office as early as 5:00 AM."

- Pastor Craig Groeschel
(The Thrivetime Show guest and the pastor of the largest evangelical church in America which has over 100,000 members, Life.Church)

"Early to bed and early to rise makes a man healthy, wealthy, and wise."

- Benjamin Franklin
(The polymath who was a famous inventor of the Franklin Stove, bifocals, the lightning rod, a Founding Father of the United States, the diplomat who convinced the French to save us during the revolutionary war, the best-selling author, the founder of the University of Pennsylvania and much, much, more.)

"I get up every day around 6 in the morning and I'm at work around 7:30. And that gives me about an hour before most people show up so I have some time to prepare."

- Jim Bridenstein
(The Thrivetime Show guest and the head of NASA.)

"Usually I wake up early before 6 AM. This gives me a chance to clear my head."

- Seth Goldman
(The Thrivetime Show guest and the co-founder of Honest Tea who is the executive chairman of Beyond Meat.)

"The sun has not caught me in bed in fifty years."

- Thomas Jefferson
(One of America's Founding Fathers, the third President of the United States, the second Vice President of the United States, a lawyer, an architect and so much more.)

"During the season I normally wake up around 4:30 AM or 5:00 AM."

- Jack Easterby
(The Thrivetime Show podcast guest, and former Character Coach for the New England Patriots football team.)

"I'm up every day around 4:30 AM."

- Jason Jennings
(The Thrivetime Show guest and 6X New York Time best-selling author.)

"I wake up at 3 AM."

- Jeff Hoffman
(The Thrivetime Show guest, the best-selling author of Scale and a key founding member of Priceline.com)

"I get up at 5:00 AM most days."

- Jay Papasan
(The Thrivetime Show guest and New York Times best-selling author of The One Thing that he co-wrote with the co-founder of Keller Williams Gary Keller.)

"I get to the office everyday at 6:15 AM. I use that time to plan my day."

- Lee Cockerell
(The frequent Thrivetime Show guest and former Executive Vice President of Walt Disney World Resorts who once managed over 40,000 employees while being responsible for the satisfaction of the 1,000,000 customers per week that chose to visit the world's largest and most successful theme and amusement park)

Having interviewed thousands (literally thousands) of the world's most successful people I can tell that **ALL OF THEM** on average wake up hours before the rest of the world (other than my partner Doctor Zoellner who after working 7 days per week for years in route to his success and who is a night owl, has earned the right to stay up as late as he wants).

Although most people are obsessed with the wondering what they are going to eat each day for lunch, what the weather forecast is going to be and who is "blowing up on social media" top level entrepreneurs are always simply focused on what they can control. The top entrepreneurs, millionaires, and billionaires that we have interviewed on The Thrivetime Show podcast have universally decided that they are only going to think 100% of their thoughts about work when they are at work.

"ONE OF THE PENALTIES OF LEADERSHIP IS THE NECESSITY OF WILLINGNESS UPON THE PART OF THE LEADER TO DO MORE THAN HE REQUIRES OF HIS FOLLOWERS."
- NAPOLEON HILL
(THE AUTHOR OF THE BEST-SELLING SELF-HELP BOOK OF ALL TIME, *THINK AND GROW RICH.*)

CHAPTER 5

Focus On What You Can Control and Don't Watch
the Weather Channel When Possible.

THE WEATHER CHANNEL UNPLUGGED: LET GO OF WHAT YOU CAN'T CONTROL

Successful people have learned to focus exclusively on what they can control. In fact, just a few weeks ago, I arrived at the office at 3:45 in the morning, after driving through the snow, to knock out another productive work day. Shortly after planning out my day, I turned my smartphone on to check my messages only to discover a "flurry" of text messages coming in that said things like:

1.

Are we working today with all of that snow coming in?

2.

Are we still meeting today with the snow and all?

3.

Are you OK? I know that snow is headed your way.

4.

I can't meet today with all of the snow coming in. I want to be safe.

5.

Can we reschedule today? I don't want to risk driving in with all of the snow.

However, all of my most successful clients drove in just like I did. Do you want to know why? Successful people do not focus on what they cannot control. They do not watch the Weather Channel or the nightly news. Why? Because the daily events on the news and the weather patterns being reported rarely impact our daily lives at all. It is very easy to invest your waking hours following "the news" and politics while waving the flag that "it's important to stay informed." Yet, I will tell you this, it is better for you to spend your life creating a life that the news media would someday want to interview you about rather than to spend your precious free time watching the lives of other successful people. Don't block out time in your schedule for watching the Weather Channel and the news or you are MUCH MORE LIKELY TO LOSE. How much time each day are you focused on things you can't control? _____.

What are you going to cut out starting now? _____
_____.

CHAPTER 6

Without the Ability to Sell, Your Business
Dreams Will Go to Hell.

"EVERYTHING ELSE BECOMES UNNECESSARY IN A BUSINESS IF NOBODY SELLS ANYTHING."

- Clay Clark
(The founder DJ Connection, EITRLounge.com, EpicPhotos.com, MakeYourLifeEpic.com, etc.)

Sales is the lifeblood of your business. Without the ability to sell, you will not do well and your business will go to hell. One of the dumbest and most consistently incorrect statements I hear "wantrepreneuers," and perpetually failing business owners saying is, "This product is so good it will sell itself." That is not true. Even if your idea is world-class and a game-changer, you are going to have to learn how to sell and to sell well, if you want to **succeed** on this planet.

"IF YOU CAN'T SELL YOU MAY NOT USE THE BRIDGE TO GO OVER THE LAKE OF FIRE!"

"EXCUSE ME MR. KNIGHT. UMM, COULD I PLEASE USE YOUR BRIDGE TO CROSS OVER THE LAKE OF FIRE PLEASE?"

THE DUMBEST AND MOST CONSISTENTLY QUOTED NOTABLE QUOTABLE PHRASES ON THE PLANET:

"If you build it they will come."

- Kevin Costner,
   (From the hit movie *Field of Dreams.*)

"Create a product so good that it will sell itself."

- Someone Stupid

"NOTABLE QUOTABLES"

"Even if you have a world-class idea and want to give it away for the good of humanity, you will have to sell the concept. If you can't sell it, you'll be stuck with your idea, poorer for your brilliance and generosity. It seems unfair, but even freebies must be delivered with a certain salesmanship or the receiver does not perceive the true value of the gift. Everything has to be sold. Yet, so few people sell well that 15% of salespeople make 85% of the available money. At your next sales meeting with 20 people, three will take home the money of the 17 others. What is it that allows these three people to have that money flow their way. Is it luck, hard work and a good attitude? Or is it persuasive skill - understanding the transactional dynamics of the selling process?"

- Jerry Vass
    (Thrivetime Show guest and best-selling author of Soft Selling)

Selling is currently the highest paid profession known to mankind. Business leaders, political leaders and top religious leaders are all very skilled in the art of persuasion and sales. At some junction during their career they had to sell their vision, their product, their service or their solution to the planet in exchange for the wealth and success that they now enjoy. If you want to learn how to sell and how to sell well, the best books you can read on the subject are listed below:

1.

Soft Selling in a Hard World *by Jerry Vass.*

2.

The Ultimate Sales Machine *by Chet Holmes.*

3. ***How to Win Friends and Influence People***
by Dale Carnegie.

THE CAPACITY OF TENACITY:
OVERCOMING OBSTACLES

In order to become great at sales you must understand the following three concepts:

1.

Failure is a prerequisite to success and you must get 100 rejections for every 1 yes.

2.

Sales is a skill and the mechanics of sales can be taught and learned.

3.

Once nailed, sales systems can be scaled and large sales organizations can be built.

"THIS PRODUCT IS SO GOOD, IT WILL SELL ITSELF."
— SOMEONE STUPID

ACTION STEPS:

1.

To begin to learn the sales super moves that you can use, listen to my exclusive interview with the author of *Soft Selling in a Hard World*, Jerry Vass https://www.thrivetimeshow.com/business-podcasts/how-to-soft-sell-in-a-hard-world-with-master-sales-trainer-jerry-vass/

2.

To learn the practical sales moves that you can use to earn more money immediately, download a free ebook copy of my books by visiting: www.thrivetimeshow.com/free-resources/

NOTABLE QUOTABLE:

"Action is the real measure of intelligence."

- Napoleon Hill
(The legendary best-selling author of Think and Grow Rich.)

CHAPTER 7

Once You Nail It, You Must Scale It or to the Idea
of Time Freedom You Must Say to Hell With It!

O ne of my long-time clients and a man whom I consider to be a good friend, is the Atlantic recording singer, song-writer and chart-topping pop music artist, Colton Dixon. His work ethic is admirable, his voice is angelic and the level of skill that he has developed is approaching Elton John level. He is an artist. Colton is super skilled yet he is not scalable. He is not duplicable or repeatable on a massive scale which is what you actually want an artist to be. This is why thousands of people eagerly fill up arenas to watch Colton Dixon perform. However, in the world of entrepreneurship, if you want to create time and financial freedom, YOU MUST NAIL IT AND THEN SCALE. Once you figure out the product experience or service experience that WOWs your ideal and likely buyers, you need to create the systems, scripts, checklists, and processes needed to make your business repeatable. Ideally, you want to create systems that allow people (who are not you) to provide the level of product and service quality that you yourself would provide without actually involving any of YOUR time. YOU are not SCALABLE.

The way to start creating the scalable systems is to document everything you do in a bullet point format. Pick one item that you do consistently and document the specific steps today. What task will you document today?

Pictured above from left to right is Annie Dixon (Colton's wife), Vanessa Clark (my wife), myself, and Colton Dixon.

The pair of Yeezys that Colton sent me as a thank you gift is pictured above.

"NOTABLE QUOTABLES"

"Develop an attitude of gratitude, and give thanks for everything that happens to you, knowing that every step forward is a step toward achieving something bigger and better than your current situation."

- Brian Tracy
(The world-renowned best-selling author and legendary sales trainer.)

"I try to invest in businesses that are so wonderful that an idiot can run them. Because sooner or later, one will."

- Warren Buffett
(The billionaire investor who started with nothing, but who is now worth $90.6 billion according to Forbes despite having given away $46 billion since 2000.)

CHAPTER 8

You Must Commit to Your Business Because
Nobody Else is Going to Care as Much As You.

"PUT ALL OF YOUR EGGS IN ONE BASKET, AND WATCH THAT BASKET."
- ANDREW CARNEGIE
(THE SELF-MADE STEEL TYCOON AND PHILANTHROPIST)

When you build a business, you must be 100% committed to it because nobody else is. When I first started DJConnection.com, I thought I would start it with some college friends. However, one by one they couldn't make it. They were running behind, something came up, or they flaked out on me for one reason or another. When I built my first photography and videography company, I thought that I would start this business with friends, but they just couldn't get the projects done, had a vacation that got in the way of delivering what we promised to our paying

customers or they didn't feel like it was worth their time. Thus, at the end of the day, it has always come down to me, and this story will be the same for you and your business as you attempt to grow it and you already know it. It would be nice if other people or anyone would come along and care about your business as much as you do, but more than likely it is not going to happen. Thus, you must understand that YOU must commit to your business as though your life depends on it.

"
NOTABLE
QUOTABLES
"

"A long while ago, a great warrior faced a situation which made it necessary for him to make a decision which insured his success on the battlefield. He was about to send his armies against a powerful foe, whose men outnumbered his own. He loaded his soldiers into boats, sailed to the enemy's country, unloaded soldiers and equipment, then gave the order to burn the ships that had carried them. Addressing his men before the first battle, he said, "You see the boats going up in smoke. That means that we cannot leave these shores alive unless we win! We now have no choice-we win-or we perish! They won.

Every person who wins in any undertaking must be willing to burn his ships and cut all sources of retreat. Only by so doing can one be sure of maintaining that state of mind known as a BURNING DESIRE TO WIN, essential to success."

- Napoleon Hill
  (The best-selling author of *Think and Grow Rich.*)

"Be the pig at breakfast and not the egg. A pig gave it's life for breakfast, where as a chicken only gave an egg."

- Dr. Robert Zoellner
(Co-host of The Thrivetime Show, the founder of Doctor Zoellner's Optometry, Z66 Auto Auction, an owner of BankRegent.com, etc.)

"All super successful people possess the burning maniacal passion to achieve as though their very life depended upon it."

- Michael Levine
(The Thrivetime Show guest, New York Times best-selling author and public relations consultant of choice for Michael Jackson, Prince, Nike, President Clinton, Charlton Heston, etc.)

"A well-defined backup plan is sabotage waiting to happen. Why push through the dip, why take the risk, why blow it all when there's the comfortable alternative instead? The people who break through usually have nothing to lose, and they almost never have a backup plan."

- Seth Godin
(The Thrivetime Show podcast guest and the best-selling author, entrepreneur and founder of Yoyodyne which was sold to Yahoo for $30,000,000.)

CHAPTER 9

Most People Die at the Age
of 25, But are Not Buried
Until the Age of 75.

:

"SOME PEOPLE DIE AT 25 AND AREN'T BURIED UNTIL 75."
- BENJAMIN FRANKLIN

(ONE OF THE FOUNDING FATHERS
OF THE UNITED STATES.)

Most people quit dreaming, and begin to lose hope and stop pushing forward towards their goals at or before the age of 25. Why? Success is not normal and most people are not used to the level of commitment and resilience that achieving financial and business success requires. Most people simply quit on themselves. In order for you to become successful, you must decide here and now that you will not quit UNTIL YOU GET THERE. Take the word quit out of your verbal and mental vocabulary. Commit to not stop UNTIL YOU GET THERE. Say it with me now, "I will not quit until I get there." I don't think that you believe it yet. Say it with me again now, "I will not quit UNTIL I GET THERE!"

109

"NOTABLE QUOTABLES"

"The capacity to surmount failure without being discouraged is the chief asset of every person who attains outstanding success in any calling."

- Napoleon Hill
  (The best-selling self-help author of all-time and the personal apprentice of Andrew Carnegie who was once the world's wealthiest man despite having grown up impossibly poor.)

FUN FACTS!

We talked about these sad facts earlier, but I want you to really mentally marinate on the profundity of this idea! YOU MUST REMEMBER that most people are not succeeding. I am going to try to forever sear the following facts into your brain:

➡ *Forbes* now reports that 70% of people hate their jobs.

➡ *Inc. Magazine* shares that 85% of potential employees lie on their resumes.

➡ *Inc. Magazine* reports that 96% of businesses fail within 10 years.

➡ 47% of Americans leach from the system and pay no taxes.

➡ The *Washington Post* reports that 78% of men have cheated on their spouse.

➡️ *CNN Money* now reports that 40% of Americans now have less than $400 saved.

Don't believe me? The truth hurts, but it is verifiable. Click on the links below:

➡️ https://www.forbes.com/sites/carminegallo/2011/11/11/your-emotionally-disconnected-employees/

➡️ https://www.inc.com/jt-odonnell/staggering-85-of-job-applicants-lying-on-resumes-.html

➡️ https://www.inc.com/bill-carmody/why-96-of-businesses-fail-within-10-years.html

➡️ https://www.marketwatch.com/story/81-million-americans-wont-pay-any-federal-income-taxes-this-year-heres-why-2018-04-16

➡️ https://www.washingtonpost.com/opinions/five-myths-about-cheating/2012/02/08/gIQANGdaBR_story.html?noredirect=on

➡️ https://money.cnn.com/2018/05/22/pf/emergency-expenses-household-finances/index.html

CHAPTER 10

Time is Your Most Precious Asset. You Can Always
Make More Money, But You Can't Make More Time.

"TIME IS THE SCARCEST RESOURCE OF THE MANAGER;
IF IT IS NOT MANAGED, NOTHING ELSE CAN BE MANAGED."
- PETER F. DRUCKER
MANAGEMENT CONSULTANT, EDUCATOR, AND AUTHOR

All super successful people place an enormous amount of value on their time and the time of others. Super successful people are rarely late to anything, because they don't want to waste someone else's time. Super successful people are constantly asking themselves, "Is this the best use of my time?" Super successful people will not do something just because it is free or just because somebody asked them to do it. Super successful people operate with the mantras, "You must say no to grow," and "everything that is not helping to gain traction is a distraction."

Traction is anything that moves you closer to your goals. However, distraction is anything that moves you further away from your goals. All of the super successful people that I have ever met are passionate about making sure that they are not wasting their time.

Because super successful people recognize that your network creates your net worth and that you do in fact become the average of the five people that you spend the most time with, they simply refuse to hang out with negative influences and be physically present in environments that are not lifting them to the achievement of their goals. In a world of perpetual distraction, super successful people do not waste the 13 hours per week that the average American now spends checking emails. Super successful people simply refuse to spend 11 hours per day on their smartphones operating in a state of perpetual distraction. Super successful people value their time, because they know that it is their most important asset and they simply refuse to waste it.

"NOTABLE QUOTABLES"

"Determine never to be idle. No person will have occasion to complain of the want of time who never loses any. It is wonderful how much can be done if we are always doing."

- Thomas Jefferson
(The legendary American statesman, diplomat, lawyer, architect, philosopher, and Founding Father who served as the third president of the United States from 1801 to 1809. He previously served as the second vice president of the United States from 1797 to 1801. The principal author of the Declaration of Independence.)

"Idle hands are the devil's workshop; idle lips are his mouthpiece."

- Proverbs 16:27

FUN FACTS!

→ Did you know that according to Nielsen, the average American adult now spends 11 hours per day interacting with their media?
- *https://www.nielsen.com/us/en/insights/ article/2018/time-flies-us-adults-now-spend- nearly-half-a-day-interacting-with-media*

→ "It Takes 23 Minutes to Recover From a Distraction at Work"
- *https://www.inc.com/nicholas-mcgill/it-takes- 23-minutes-to-recover-from-a-distraction-at- work-heres-how-to-minimize-.html*

→ "In June 2016, another study reported that the typical smartphone owner interacts with his or her phone an average of 85 times per day."
- *https://www.psychologytoday.com/us/blog/ the-athletes-way/201706/are-smartphones- making-us-stupid*

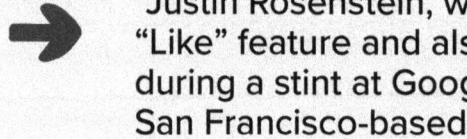 "Justin Rosenstein, who created Facebook's "Like" feature and also helped create Gchat during a stint at Google, and now leads a San Francisco-based company that improves office productivity, appears most concerned about the psychological effects on people who, research shows, touch, swipe or tap their phone 2,617 times a day."
- *https://www.theguardian.com/ technology/2017/oct/05/smartphone- addiction-silicon-valley-dystopia*

 "The average worker spends 51% of each workday on these 3 unnecessary tasks."
- *https://www.inc.com/geoffrey-james/the- average-worker-spends-51-of-each-workday- on-these-3-unnecessary-tasks.html*

CHAPTER 11

It's All About Resourcefulness and Not About Resources. Start Now With What You Have. The Time Will Never Be Just Right.

The 1984 chevy brown van is a doorless vehicle that I famously drove for nearly 5 years.

You and I don't need to spend thousands of dollars on an super expensive auto wrap to start a successful plumbing business. You don't need to do a custom-coded website to start a successful real estate company. You don't need brand new work trucks on massive lift kits with oversized tires to start a roofing company.

When I started one of the largest wedding entertainment companies that went on to provide entertainment for over 4,000 events per year (DJConnection.com), I was driving a 1989 Ford Escort with nearly 200,000 miles on it. I could not afford to autowrap it, but I wanted my vehicle to generate leads and awareness around the college campus of Oral Roberts University, that there was DJ on campus. So, I hand-painted the vehicle. Hand-painted? Yep. I used the One Shot Lettering Enamel which was designed for sign painters and I made it happen. Was it ideal? No. Did it work? Yes. Within weeks of enrolling at Oral Roberts University, everybody knew my name and they knew my game (the DJ service that I could provide).

My 1989 hand-painted Ford Escort is pictured below.

Most people never start their business because they make excuses and say:

- I would start a business if I was a little younger.

- I will start a business after I graduate from college.

- I will start a business after I get married.

- I will start a business after I go back and get my MBA.

- I will start a business after we have kids.

- I will start a business if I can just raise $100,000 of venture capital.

- I will start a business after _____.

In this life there is no "Someday" on our calendars. We only have Monday, Tuesday, Wednesday, Thursday, Friday, Saturday, and Sunday. The time is never going to be ideal. If you are going to start, you must start now.

"The time will never be just right. You must act now."

- Napoleon Hill
(The best-selling author of *Think and Grow Rich*.)

"DON'T LET SCHOOLING INTERFERE WITH YOUR EDUCATION."
- MARK TWAIN, AMERICAN AUTHOR

> "The way to get started is to quit talking and begin doing."

> — Walt Disney
> (The legendary co-founder of the Disney Empire who went bankrupt in 1923 at the age of 22, but who refused to allow previous failure stop him.)

132

Don't over complicate this. Remember, starting a business just requires finding a problem that you can solve for other humans that they are actually willing to pay you to solve. Don't get stuck! Get started:

What are some problems that you could solve that people would be willing to pay for?

1. _____

2. _____

3. _____

133

"NOTABLE QUOTABLES"

"Ninety-nine percent of the failures come from people who have the habit of making excuses."

- George Washington Carver
(A man who was born a slave, yet went on to become America's leading agricultural scientist. George Washington Carver recognized that the newly freed slaves were aggressively depleting their soil of nutrients by perpetually planting only cotton, thus he was determined to solve the problem. George Washington Carver knew that planting sweet potatoes and peanuts into the soil would restore minerals and nutrients to the soil, but he knew that there really wasn't a huge market for sweet potatoes or peanuts. So what did he do? He obsessively focused on developing financially viable products that could be made using sweet potatoes and peanuts. It was George Washington Carver who was responsible for returning fertility to the soil and allowing his newly freed people to become financially free.)

CHAPTER 12

Don't Ask Most People for Advice and Don't Listen
to Their Unsolicited Advice

"GREAT SPIRITS HAVE ALWAYS ENCOUNTERED VIOLENT OPPOSITION FROM MEDIOCRE MINDS."
– ALBERT EINSTEIN

(The man responsible for developing the nuclear weapons we used to destroy the Japanese and the Nazis who were maniacally focused on taking over the free world and eliminating Jewish people from the planet.)

As discussed throughout this book, most people are wrong about most things most of the time. These people are going the wrong way in the game life. However, not only are they going the wrong way, but they are also very passionate about taking you with them. Misery loves company. Idiots who are losing in the game of life, love to provide entrepreneurs, like you and me, with bad advice. Throughout my career, I have had to constantly battle with employees, competitors, business people, and family about the topic of staying the course and turning my dreams into reality. When I started DJConnection.com out of my college dorm room, everybody kept asking me what my backup plan was. When I started hiring employees they would argue with me about the ethics of cold-calling, and about how our trade show booth should be set up.

Employees would argue with me about the hours I needed them to work and they would argue about their pay. Once they finished arguing about their pay, they would start arguing about why they didn't get promoted. If they did get promoted they would argue with me about why the other employees didn't respect them. As an entrepreneur you have to resolve in your mind that fighting is your new normal.

— — — — — — — — — —

"NOTABLE QUOTABLES"

"You are just going to go from fighting at this level to fighting at that level. The fight will always continue. Big church. Little church. Lots of money. No money. There is always something that fights you back because strength is developed through resistance. Stop crying about what you are going through. If it ain't this it's going to be that. So I used the strength from the struggle I had against the struggle I have right now. The Bible says it was good for me that I was afflicted. That's why the Devil can't chase me out of town because of a fight. I cut my teeth in a fight. You just have to make up your mind that fighting is normal. Let me tell you how I always know that I am going to have a MOMENT. Whenever I'm about to have a MOMENT, I always have an attack."

- T.D. Jakes
(The iconic pastor, author and filmmaker. He is the pastor of The Potter's House, a non-denominational American mega church.)

"Optimism, pessimism, f@#* that; we're going to make it happen. As God is my bloody witness, I'm hell-bent on making it work."

- Elon Musk
   (The self-made billionaire man behind Zip2, SpaceX, Tesla, SolarCity, PayPal, etc.)

To encourage you, I have put together a list of people who had to fight through crazy adversity in route to building the careers and brands that we all now know:

- **NFL Great, James Harrison** - Before becoming the NFL's Defensive Player of the Year, James Harrison was cut from an NFL team four times and three of those times by the Steelers. James Harrison became a five-time Pro Bowl selection, and he won two Super Bowls with the Steelers: XL and XLIII. In 2008, he became the only undrafted player to be named Associated Press NFL Defensive Player of the Year.

- **Amazon.com** was started by Jeff Bezos in 1994 out of his garage. In 1999 he lost $719 million. It took Jeff 9 years to turn a profit in 2003.

- **ESPN -** ESPN was founded in 1978, yet the company did not make a profit until the mid 1990s.

- **Tesla** --Tesla was founded in June of 2003 by Martin Eberhard, yet it took Tesla over 10 years to turn a profit.

- **Dyson Vacuums** - It took James Dyson 15 years to create his first Dual Cyclone vacuum cleaner, which did not hit stores until 1993. He created 5,126 versions that failed before he actually created a prototype that worked.

- **Thomas Edison** - Thomas Edison created 10,000 failed experiments of the lightbulb before he created one that actually worked.

The Mindset of
THOMAS EDISON

"TEMPORARY FAILURES ARE A PREREQUISITE TO SUCCESS."
–NAPOLEON HILL
BEST–SELLING SUCCESS AUTHOR OF *"THINK AND GROW RICH"*

- **Reddit** - When Alexis Ohanian and the Reddit founders started Reddit in 2005, very few people were using the platform, so they created fake accounts to make it look like they had a bunch of traffic. Using their bogus accounts, they worked to create the overall tonality and direction of the discussions that were on the website. Once traffic grew to a certain size, they no longer continued using the fake accounts.

- **AirBNB** - The founders of AirBnB secured their initial funding as a result of creating and selling their own cereal. They actually bought large amounts of bulk cereal and put together cardboard boxes, and created limited edition brands of politically themed cereals called Cap'n McCain and Obama O's and the Breakfast of Change. In less than 60 days they sold 800 boxes of cereal for $40 a piece to generate over $30,000. They later commented that they had big success selling the Obama themed cereal, but they ended up eating the McCain cereal as food since they couldn't sell it very easily.

- **Google** – Larry Page and Sergey Brin started working on Google in 1996 – but three years later in 1999, few people had even heard of it yet. – http://www.businessinsider.com/guess-how-long-overnight-success-really-takes-2011-3

- **Facebook** – While attending Harvard as a sophomore, Mark Zuckerberg concocted "Facemash" in 2003 to get a lost girlfriend off his mind. He later changed the name to Facebook. In 2005, Facebook still showed a yearly net loss of $3.63 million. – http://www.businessinsider.com/guess-how-long-overnight-success-really-takes-2011-3

- **Walt Disney** - In route to building the Disney empire, the great Walt Disney lost it all twice.

- **Ford Automotive** - On his path to making the automobile affordable to nearly all Americans, Henry Ford lost it all five times.

CHAPTER 13

Measure What You Treasure, Track Reality and
Don't Run Your Business Based Upon Projections.

"FACE REALITY AS IT IS, NOT AS IT WAS
OR AS YOU WISH IT TO BE."
- JACK WELCH
FORMER CEO OF GENERAL ELECTRIC

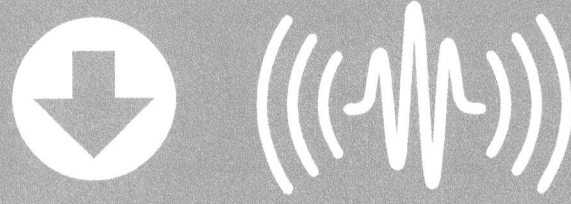

As an entrepreneur you must be filled with faith, but you must also track reality. As a business owner you must be fired up with belief, but you must also balance the budget. As a self-

DON'T STOP. KEEP MOVING THROUGH THE FOG UNTIL YOU SEE THE LIGHT.

FEAR

CONFUSION

PAIN

DOUBT

employed person you must burn the boats and operate as though your very life depended upon the success of the business, but you must also not reject math.

So many entrepreneurs are too FIRED UP, PUMPED UP, and HIGHLY CAFFEINATED to ever look at their numbers until their checks start to bounce, creditors start calling, and they find themselves having to explain to their spouse why the bank is going to be taking back their house.

Far too often (especially with contractors) I see entrepreneurs who want to exclusively focus on the offensive side of the business. For some reason they have a DANGEROUS SELF-SABOTAGING REFUSAL TO EVER LOOK AT THEIR NUMBERS BECAUSE "they have an accountant who handles that!" You can delegate, but you cannot abdicate your finances. Amen.

THE DEFINITION MAGICIAN:

 - **Delegation** is when you clearly assign a specific task with a specific deadline and you follow up with this person to verify that the task got done.

 - **Abdication** is what used to happen when a King was on the verge of being overthrown. Back in the day, the King would abdicate the throne, which was the act of formally relinquishing their power and giving it to somebody else so that they wouldn't get killed by the person who wanted their job and title as King.

 - **Determination -** Don't blindly hand over your finances to "some dude" or to "some accounting service" or to "some bookkeeping service" based upon your delusional beliefs that they are going to care about your finances as much as you do.

> "Don't ever let your business get ahead of the financial side of your business. Accounting, accounting, accounting. Know your numbers."

— Tilman Fertitta

(The businessman and television personality. He is the chairman, CEO, and sole owner of Landry's, Inc., one of the largest restaurant corporations in the U.S. He also owns the National Basketball Association (NBA)'s Houston Rockets. His net worth was estimated at $4.5 billion, placing him at No. 153 on the Forbes 400 list of the wealthiest Americans; Forbes calls him the "World's Richest Restaurateur.")

I have seen WAY TOO MANY ENTREPRENEURS finding themselves in a spot where they owe our good friends at the Internal Revenue Service a massive amount of taxes simply because they abdicated their finances for a year. I've also met many people that have unfortunately found themselves as the proud owners of a piece of real estate that is hemorrhaging money and that does not have the ability to ever become the income producing property that they

For Sale
All American House
Only After Interest
30% Larger

Today's Price
$272,900

Insert Money Here

thought it was going to be when they bought it. Why? The devil is in the details. The difference between success and failure is most often determined by the level of intensity you are willing to put into thoroughly reading contracts, analyzing deals, and searching passionately for those deal-breaking details found inside the contracts that somebody is trying to screw you over with.

A business is like a garden and YOU must tend to it. Pull the weeds when you see them. You can't look at your finances once per month and call it good.

IT'S NOT ABOUT HOW MUCH YOU MAKE,
ITS ABOUT HOW MUCH YOU KEEP.
-CLAY CLARK

ACTION STEPS:

1.

Schedule a specific time each and every week to look at your finances. In this financial meeting:

2.

Look at your actual bank balance (don't hide from it).

3.

Look at all of your actual expenses.

4.

Look at all of your actual income streams.

5.

Ask yourself, "how can you reduce your expenses by 3% this week?"

6.

Ask yourself, "how can you increase your profits by 1% this week?"

7.

Automate the saving of a minimum of 5% of your income.

"NOTABLE QUOTABLES"

"Remember, inspiration unused is merely entertainment. To get new results, you need to take new actions."

- David Bach
(The 9X New York Times best-selling author of The Automatic Millionaire: A Powerful One-Step Plan to Live and Finish Rich)

CHAPTER 14

Stop Guessing, Hoping, Wishing and Praying for Directions. Use MAPs, GPS, and Guides That Have Clearly Demonstrated That They Know the Proven Path

You would never attempt to drive 12 hours to a legendary vacation destination that you have never been to without using a map, or a GPS (global positioning system), so why would you attempt to grow your business via guess-work? Building a business that works is not a magical or mystical thing based upon serendipity and luck. Constructing a building that does not fall down is not based upon luck. Building an automobile that works efficiently is not a mystical thing based upon luck, randomness, and guess work. Doctor Zoellner and I have been able to build 16 multi-million dollar companies between the two of us. Mentally marinate on that fact for a moment. Look up some of the successful ventures that either he or I have built, alphabetically speaking:

- BankRegent.com

- DJConnection.com

- DrZoellner.com

- EpicPhotos.com

- MakeYourLifeEpic.com

- TipTopK9.com (I am a partner with this company and have helped Rachel and Ryan Wimpey to scale and franchise their business, but I did not start it).

- Z66AA.com

Why haven't we declared bankruptcy? Why haven't our businesses ever failed?

- We follow a proven plan.

- We won't stop until we achieve success.

So what if you don't have a proven plan? Find someone who knows the way up the proven path to success.

"NOTABLE QUOTABLES"

"Most people are too indifferent or lazy to acquire FACTS with which to THINK ACCURATELY. They prefer to act on "opinions" created by guesswork or snap-judgments."

- Napoleon Hill
  (The best-selling self-help author of all-time and the man who wrote the legendary book, *Think and Grow Rich.*)

"Most of the time when you get people coming up for prayer it's always about money. Our mentality is that we need a miracle. I'm believing God for a car. I'm believing God for a house. I'm believing God for a coat. I'm believing God to send my kids to private school. I hate to tell you this. There are atheists that send their kids to private school. There are drug dealers that have a car. That's not a miracle. You don't need God. You need a good job. You need to come to work. You need to save your money. You can get yourself a car. You don't need to call on heaven and provoke the angels to get a car. That magical mentality is killing the church. We are asking God for stuff that we can do ourselves."

- Bishop T.D. Jakes
(Excerpt from his It's Not For Sale sermon that he delivered on December 29th of 2019)

"MOST ENTREPRENEURS ARE MERELY TECHNICIANS WITH AN ENTREPRENEURIAL SEIZURE. MOST ENTREPRENEURS FAIL BECAUSE THEY ARE WORKING IN THEIR BUSINESS RATHER THAN ON THEIR BUSINESS."
- MICHAEL GERBER
(AUTHOR OF "THE E-MYTH REVISITED")

Where can you find people that know the proven path?

1.

If you are stuck with your accounting, find an accountant with a proven track record of success. Call their actual references and their current clients to verify that the accountant does what they say they are is going to do.

2.

If you are stuck with the legal aspects of your business visit www.WintersKing.com. These guys are my legal counsel and they have or currently represent many businesses and personalities that you would know including the founder of Life.Church, Pastor Craig Groeschel, the legendary pastor, best-selling author and entrepreneur, Bishop T.D. Jakes, the Pastor of Lakewood Church, Joel Osteen, the incredible female pastor who is on a mission, Joyce Meyer, etc. Specifically when you reach out to Winters and King, ask for Wes Carter. He is a partner and is my attorney. And NO, I am not legally allowed to receive pay to encourage you to use his services. However, I have asked.

3.

In a world where Inc. Magazine reports that 96% of businesses will fail within 10 years, why did my average client grow by 104% in 2019? Don't believe me? Check out the following links:

www.ThrivetimeShow.com/testimonials

www.ThrivetimeShow.com/does-it-work

As you watch the video testimonials, read the verifiable growth numbers, and hear the stories from people that look just like you and who don't come from privilege. You must ask yourself why aren't you thriving and growing your business rapidly? Bottom line, you aren't growing because you either don't know the way or you aren't willing to implement the proven path that has been shown to you. My mission is to mentor millions and that includes you. Schedule your 13 point consultation with me (actually me, not Robert Kiyosaki's Rich Dad advisors, or somebody I know). During this consultation we will find out where you are stuck and then if you are a good fit I will invest the 3 to 4 hours needed to create a customized business plan / path just for you.

PLOT YOUR COURSE OR YOU WILL NEVER GET THERE

As a business coach, I am exclusively focused on results and not feelings, which is why I feel good about the results of the clients I will list on the following pages. However, as a cautionary note, I only take on 160 clients at any given time. Why? Because I write all of the business plans and I personally conduct each and every client's 13-point assessment. To put this in perspective, every week we have dozens and sometimes hundreds of people who reach out for one-on-one business coaching, yet I only say yes to a client about once per month because I never want to coach more than 160 clients. Why? Business coaching is my art, it is my passion, it is my soul and it is intentionally not a scalable business model. Listed are our documented client success stories from 2018-2019 in the next several pages:

FUN
FACTS!

It's worth repeating and dwelling on over and over until your brain explodes and you get this truth permanently plastered inside of your cranium. By default, according to *Inc. Magazine*, 96% of businesses fail within 10 years and my clients average a 104% growth rate. Is it luck? No. Is it a spiritual victory over Satan? No. Is it because I work closely with the Illuminati to control markets? No. Our clients win because I know the proven plan and only allow diligent doers into our one-on-one coaching program.

 By default 96% of businesses fail and our clients grow on average of 104% per year.

And now without any further ado...I present to you documented success stories.

A Better Plumber
Jeff Watson
www.ABetterPlumberCo.com
2018 - 2019 Up 79%

Accolade Exteriors
Stuart Weikel
www.AccoladeExteriors.com
2018 - 2019 Up 82%

Amy Baltimore, CPA
Amy Baltimore
www.AmyBaltimoreCPA.com
2018 - 2019 Up 34%

Angel's Touch
Christina Nemes
www.CapeCodAutoBodyandDetailing.com
2018 - 2019 Up 67%

Back to Basics Builders
Joe Burbey
www.HomeRemodelingMilwaukee.com
2018 - 2019 Up 35%

Best Buy Window Treatment
Ergun Aral
www.BestBuyWindowTreatments.com
2018 - 2019 Up 76%

Bigfoot Restoration
Marc Lucero & Stephen Small
www.BigFootRestoration.com
2018 - 2019 Up 112%

Bogard and Sons Construction
Andy Bogard
www.BogardandSons.com
2018 - 2019 Up 32%

Breakout Creative
Chris De Jesus
www.BreakOutCreativeCompany.com
Up 59% Total

Brian T. Armstrong Construction Incorporated
Brian T. Armstrong
www.BrianTArmstrongConstructionInc.com
2017 - 2018 Up 29%
2018 - 2019 Up 89%

C&R Contracting
Ryan Kilday
www.ColoradoContracting.com
2018 - 2019 Up 240%

Catalyst Communication
Adam Duran
www.CatalystCommunicationsGroupInc.com
2018 - 2019 Up 44%

Chaney Construction
Jim and Amy Chaney
www.ChaneyConstructionTX.com
2018 - 2019 Up 19%

Citywide Mechanical
Terrance Thomas
www.CityWide-Mechanical.com
2018 - 2019 Up 118%

CK Electric
Chad Kudlacek
www.CKElectricOmaha.com
2018 - 2019 Up 25%

Colaw Fitness
Charles and Amber Colaw
www.ColawFitness.com
2018 - 2019 Up 15%

Compass Roofing
Robert Alsbrooks & Sonny Ordonez
www.CompassRoofing.com
2018 - 2019 Up 103%

Complete Carpet
Nathan & Toni Sevrinus
www.CompleteCarpetTulsa.com
2017 - 2019 Up 298%

Comfort Pro
Steve Bagwell
www.ComfortPro-Inc.com
2018 - 2019 Up 28%

CT Tech
Christopher Tracy
www.CTTec.net
2018 - 2019 Up 77%

Curtis Music
Ron Curtis
www.CurtisMusicAcademy.com
2018 - 2019 Up 58%

Custom Automation Technologies Incorporated
Dan Hoehnen
www.CustomAutomationTech.com
2018 - 2019 Up 16%

D&D Custom Homes
Dave Tucker
www.MidSouthHomeBuilder.com
2018 - 2019 Up 45%

Da Vinci
Josh Fellman and Jerome Garrett
www.500KMSP.com
2018 - 2019 Up 1,097%

Danco
Denise Richter
www.DancoPump.com
2018 - 2019 Up 17%

Delricht Research
Tyler and Rachel Hastings
www.DelrichtResearch.com
2018 - 2019 Up 300%

Dr. Breck Kasbaum Chiropractor
Dr. Breck Kasbaum
www.DrBreck.com
2018 - 2019 Up 50%

Dynamic Electrical Solutions
Edward Durant
www.DynaElec.com
2018 - 2019 Up 16%

ECS Electric
James Crews
www.ECSElectricllc.com
2018 - 2019 Up 26%

Edmond Dental
Dr. Joseph Tucker
www.EdmondDentalatDeerCreek.com
2018 - 2019 Up 205%

Electrical Investments
James Henry
www.ElectricalInvestments.com
2018 - 2019 Up 21%

EnviZion Insurance
Austin Grieci
www.EZInsurancePlan.com
2018 - 2019 Up 800%

Full Package Media
Thomas James Crosson
www.FullPackageMedia.com
2018 - 2019 Up 15%

Gable's Excavating Incorporated
Levi Gable
www.GEI-USA.com
2018 - 2019 Up 66%

The Garage
Roy Coggeshall
www.TheGarageBA.com
2018 - 2019 Up 19%
2017 - Present Up 70%

The Grill Gun
Bob Healey
www.GrillBlazer.com
From Idea to Manufactured Product
8,725 Funders
Raised $920,009.00 Crowd Funding the Invention
2018 - 2019

H2Oasis Float Center
Debra Worthington
www.H2OasisFloatCenter.com
2017 - 2018 Up 17% Total

Handy Bros Services
David Visser
www.HandyBros-Services.com
2018 - 2019 Up 136%

HealthRide
Ryan Graff
www.HealthRideTulsa.org
2018 - 2019 Up 10%

Healthworks Chiropractic
Jay Schroeder
www.HealthworksChiropractic.net
2018 - 2019 Up 24%

Hood and Associates CPA's, PC
Paul Hood
www.HoodCPAs.com
2018 - 2019 Up 61%

The Hub Gym
Luke Owens
www.TheHubGym.com
2018 - 2019 Up 66.38%

Impressions Painting
Manuel Mora
www.ImpressionsPaintingTulsa.com
2018 - 2019 Up 41%

Inspired Spaces
Josh Fellman and Jerome Garrett
www.InspiredSpacesOK.com
2018 - 2019 Up 40%

Jameson Fine Cabinetry
Jamie Fagel
www.JamesonFineCabinetry.com
2018 - 2019 Up 31%

Jean Briese
Jean Briese
www.JeanBriese.com
2018 - 2019 Up 90%

KAE Edward Plumbing
Ron & Jacqueline Mader
www.KaeEdwardPlumbing.com
2018 - 2019 Up 46%

Kelly Construction Group
Jon Kelly
www.KellyConstructionGroup.com
2018 - 2019 Up 42%

Kona Honu
Byron Kay
www.KonaHonuDivers.com
2018 - 2019 Up 14%

Kurb to Kitchen
Lonny & Rinda Myers
www.KurbtoKitchenLLC.com
2018 - 2019 Up 126%

Kvell Fitness & Nutrition
Brett Denton
www.KvellFit.com
2018-2019 Up 35%+

Lake Martin Mini Mall
Jason Lett
www.LakeMartinCubed.com
2018 - 2019 Up 13%

Lakeshore Plumbing
Mike Boulte
www.LakeShorePlumbingOKC.com
2018 - 2019 Up 100%

Laundry Barn
Josh Fellman
www.TheLaundryBarn.com
2018 - 2019 Up 100%

Living Water Irrigation
Josh Wilson
www.LivingWaterIrrigationOK.com
2017 - 2019 Up 600%

Mennis Heating
Mike Ennis
www.MennisHeatingandCooling.com
2018 - 2019 Up 400%

Metal Roof Contractors
Doug Yarholar
www.MetalRoofContractorsOK.com
2018 - 2019 Up 14%

Mod Scenes
Steven Hall
www.ModScenes.com
2018 - 2019 Up 83%

Morrow, Lai and Kitterman Pediatric Dentistry
Dr. Mark Morrow, Dr. April Lai, and Dr. Kerry Kitterman
www.MLKDentistry.com
2018 - 2019 Up 42%

Mr. Rooter
Joshua Creasy
www.MrRooter.com/New-Braunfels/
2018 - 2019 Up 75%

Multi-Clean
Kevin Thomas
www.MultiCleanOK.com
2018 - 2019 Up 14%

OK Roof Nerds
Marty Grisham
www.OKRoofNerds.com
2018 - 2019 Up 74%

One Way Plumbing
Chad Ward
www.OneWayPlumbing.biz
2018 - 2019 Up 11%

Oxi Fresh
Jonathan Barnett
Matt Kline - Franchise Developer
www.OxiFresh.com
2007 to 2019 - 400 Locations Opened

Pappagallo's Pizza
Dave Rich
www.Pappagallos.com
2018 - 2019 Up 21%

Platinum Pest
Jennifer and Jared Johnson
www.Platinum-PestControl.com
2018-2019 - 25% Growth
2017-2018 - 43% Growth

PMH OKC
Randy Antrikan
www.PMHOKC.com
2018 - 2019 Up 70%

Precision Calibration
Nathan Saylor
www.PrecisionCalibrations.com
2018 - 2019 Up 62%

Quality Surfaces
John Cook
www.QualitySurfacesln.com
2018 - 2019 Up 84%

RC Auto Specialists
Roy Coggeshall
www.RCAutoSpecialists.com
2018 - 2019 Up 9%

Rescue Roofer TX
Wesley Cannon
www.RoofingDenton.com
2018 - 2019 Up 79%

Revitalize Medical Spa
Lindsey Blankenship and Crista Hobbs
www.RevitalizeMedicalSpa.com
2018 - 2019 Up 36%

Roofing & Siding Smiths
Zach Potts
www.RoofingandSidingSmiths.com
2018 - 2019 Up 67%

Rogers Plumbing
Roger Patterson
www.CallRogersPlumbing.com
2018 - 2019 Up 33%

Scotch Construction
Tim Scotch
www.ScotchConstruction.com
2017 - 2019 Up 492%

Shaw Homes
Aaron Antis
www.ShawHomes.com
2018 - 2019 Up 116%

"NOTABLE QUOTABLES"

"A Carnegie or a Rockefeller or a James J. Hill or a Marshall Field accumulates a fortune through the applications of the same principles available to all of us, but we envy them and their wealth without ever thinking of studying their philosophy and applying it to ourselves. We look at a successful person in the hour of their triumph and wonder how they did it, but we overlook the importance of analyzing their methods. And we forget the price they had to pay in the careful, well-organized preparation that had to be made before they could reap the fruits of their efforts."

- Napoleon Hill
  (The best-selling self-help author
  of all-time)

Snow Bear Air
Daniel Ramos
www.SnowBearAir.com
2018 - 2019 Up 41%

Spot-On Plumbing
Brandon Brown
www.SpotOnPlumbingTulsa.com
2018 - 2019 Up 120%

Spurrell & Associates Chartered Professional Accountants
Josh Spurrell
www.Spurrell.ca
2018 - 2019 Up 50%

Struct Construction
Brandon Haaga
www.StructConstruction.com
2018 - 2019 Up 60%

Tesla Electric
Felix Keil
www.TeslaElectricColorado.com
2018 - 2019 Up 60%

Tip Top K9
Ryan and Rachel Wimpey
www.TipTopK9.com
Grown from 1 Location - 10 Locations

Trinity Employment
Cory Minter
www.TrinityEmployment.com
2018-2019 Up 35%

Turley Solutions & Innovations
Rance Turley
www.TSI.lc
2018 - 2019 Up 300%

Sierra Pools
Cody Albright
www.SierraPoolsandSpas.com
2017 - 2019 Up 309%

Tuscaloosa Ophthalmology
Doctor Timothy Johnson
www.TTownEyes.com
2018 - 2019 Up 16%

Viva Med
Chris Lacroix
www.MyVivaMed.com
2018 - 2019 Up 90%

Veteran Home Exterior
James Peterson
www.VeteranHomeExterior.com
2018 - 2019 Up 145%

White Glove Auto
Myron Kirkpatrick
www.WhiteGloveAutoTulsa.com
2018 - 2019 - 27%

Williams Contracting
Travis Williams
www.Will-Con.com
2018 - 2019 Up 33%

Witness Security
Keith Schultz
www.WitnessLLC.com
2017 - 2019 Up 300%

CHAPTER 15

Recognize That Action is the Real
Measure of Intelligence.

"ACTION IS THE REAL MEASURE OF INTELLIGENCE."
– NAPOLEON HILL
(BEST-SELLING SUCCESS AUTHOR OF *THINK AND GROW RICH.*)

I recognize that what I am about to write flies in the face of what you have been taught by most people during most of your life, however, most people are wrong about most things most of the time.

Growing a successful business is not complicated, or something that only super intelligent people can do. Over the years, I have taught many ordinary people how to do extraordinary things. But here's the secret, you don't have to go to business college to learn these proven systems. In fact, if you go to most business colleges, you will be less likely to succeed. Academics and most business colleges teach you the EXACT OPPOSITE of the action steps that you need to take to start and grow a time and financial freedom creating business. If you want to earn both time and financial freedom you must sit down and determine your F6 goals for your life and what it will cost you per year to achieve these goals. Take the time right now to write down your F6 goals.

Faith goals #1: _____

Family goals #2: _____

Financial goals #3: _____

Fitness goals #4: _____

Friendship goals #5: _____

Fun goals #6: _____

You Don't Need a Degree to Become a Barista, But Here's Why Your Barista Probably Has a College Degree.

https://www.inc.com/suzanne-lucas/why-that-barista-has-a-college-degree-grade-inflation.html

Now invest the time needed to sit down and to determine what it will cost you on an annual basis to live the lifestyle that you want. If you want to travel constantly, what will that cost you per year? If you want to send your kids to private school, what will that cost you on an annual basis? Ask yourself if you actually need to go to college in order to do what you want to do.

Don't buy into the B.S. that you need to go to college for "the experience." Some of the dumbest days and nights of my life were spent in college hanging around people who were constantly planning what they were going to do on the weekend. Any brain power they had was spent trying to figure out their plans during "Fall Break," during "Winter Break," and during "Spring Break" when not drinking, playing video games, and attending study groups where the only thing that wasn't being done was studying.

FUN FACT:

The latest student loan debt statistics for 2019 show how serious the student loan debt crisis has become for borrowers across all demographics and age groups. There are more than 44 million borrowers who collectively owe $1.5 trillion in student loan debt in the U.S. alone. Student loan debt is now the second-highest consumer debt category – behind only mortgage debt – and higher than both credit cards and auto loans. Borrowers in the Class of 2017, on average, owe $28,650, according to the Institute for College Access and Success.

https://www.forbes.com/sites/ zackfriedman/2019/02/25/student-loan-debt- statistics-2019/#7ed5bf10133f

FUN FACT:

As of 2019, the cost to attend Oral Roberts University is $41,054 per year and the cost to attend the University of Tulsa is $59,435 per year. That is an epic waste of 4 years of your life and a life changing amount of money. Consider this, you could start a heating and air-conditioning company for $50,000 that would produce you and your family an annual income of $200,000. During your freshman year at Oral Roberts University you are going to learn about cuneiform, papyrus, the Mesopotamian Empire, and other random crap that is 100% non-practical 100% of the time. It's almost criminal how little you get in exchange for the hard earned money that people are investing into earning college degrees.

"University administrators are the equivalent of subprime mortgage brokers selling you a story that you should go into debt massively, that it's not a consumption decision, it's an investment decision. Actually, no, it's a bad consumption decision. Most colleges are four-year parties."

- Peter Thiel
(The billionaire investor behind PayPal and Facebook) https://www.businessinsider.com/peter-thiel-quotes-2014-1

Write out a list of problems that you plan on solving for ideal and likely buyers in exchange for the amount of compensation you are seeking.

Here are some examples:

1. People are hungry

2. People don't want to cut their grass

3. People don't want to haul off their own hay

4. People don't want to walk their dogs

5. People want to get from A to B and don't want to own a car

6. People in country clubs want somebody to hand them soap and mints

7. People shoot compelling videos to market their business

8. People want a container to hold gas

9. People don't want to cut their own hair

10. _____

11. _____

12. _____

13. _____

14. _____

15. _____

16. _____

17. _____

"Today if your kid wants to go to college or become a plumber, you've got to think long and hard...If he's not going to go to a great school and he's not super smart academically, but is smart in terms of dealing with people and that sort of thing, being a plumber is a great job because you have pricing power, you have an enormous skill set."

- Michael Bloomberg
  (The self-made billionaire worth an approximate $61.7 billion who was the mayor of New York City from 2002 to 2013. He is currently a candidate in the Democratic Party primaries for the 2020 United States presidential election.)

Ask yourself if you need a degree to solve the problems you want to solve. Obviously, you must earn a degree to become a:

1. Doctor

2. Lawyer

3. Dentist

4. Etc.

For a good look into the absolute waste of time that is the college experience for most people, just Google search "The General Education Classes Taught at Oral Roberts University." Are you kidding me? Why don't we replace "Humanities" with "How Google Works and How to Optimize a Website?" Why don't we replace "Quantitative Literacy" with "How to Sell Something to Another Human on the Planet Earth?" Here's an idea, let's replace anything related to studying the Mesopotamia River Valley with "How to Manage Your Time" and "How to Start a Successful Business."
http://www.oru.edu/academics/catalog/2017-18/course-descriptions.php

Why Don't Colleges Teach What Matters?

By and large, colleges don't teach you how to start or grow time and financial freedom creating businesses because the professors teaching on college campuses do not know how to start and grow a successful business. Thus, professors stand on college campuses to hide. They hide from the world of commerce where their theoretical discoveries, and hypothesis that are of no-practical value to the people of the earth, can be celebrated, subsidized and praised.

- - - - - - - - - -

"Action is the real measure of intelligence."

- Napoleon Hill
(The best-selling self-help author of all-time.)

"An educated man is one who has so developed the faculties of his mind that he may acquire anything he wants, or its equivalent, without violating the rights of others. Henry Ford comes well within the meaning of this definition."

- Napoleon Hill
  (The father of the self-help genre.)

- - - - - - - - - - - - - -

"The only thing that interferes with my learning is my education."

- Albert Einstein
  (The Nobel Prize winning physicist who introduced the concept of developing an atomic weapon to President Roosevelt. This is the reason that all Americans are not speaking German or Japanese today.)

FUN FACTS!

➡️ *Forbes* now reports that 70% of people hate their jobs

➡️ *Inc. Magazine* shares that 85% of potential employees lie on their resumes

➡️ *Inc. Magazine* reports that 96% of businesses fail within 10 years

➡️ 47% of Americans leach from the system and pay no taxes

➡️ *The Washington Post* reports that 78% of men have cheated on their spouse

➡️ *CNN Money* now reports that 40% of Americans now have less than $400 saved.

Don't believe me? The truth hurts, but it is verifiable. Click on the links below:

➡️ https://www.forbes.com/sites/carminegallo/2011/11/11/your-emotionally-disconnected-employees/

➡️ https://www.inc.com/jt-odonnell/staggering-85-of-job-applicants-lying-on-resumes-.html

➡️ https://www.inc.com/bill-carmody/why-96-of-businesses-fail-within-10-years.html

➡️ https://www.marketwatch.com/story/81-million-americans-wont-pay-any-federal-income-taxes-this-year-heres-why-2018-04-16

➡️ https://www.washingtonpost.com/opinions/five-myths-about-cheating/2012/02/08/gIQANGdaBR_story.html?noredirect=on

➡️ https://money.cnn.com/2018/05/22/pf/emergency-expenses-household-finances/index.html

You can have more degrees than a thermometer and you can have the best looking resume on the planet, but the only thing that matters in the world of business is results. In academia, you can hide from the real world and the marketplace by being good at test taking, memorizing and playing the academic game, but in the world of business, the customer is only going to keep paying you if you can solve their problems.

"NOTABLE QUOTABLES"

"As much as possible, avoid hiring MBA's. MBA programs don't teach people how to create companies ... our position is that we hire someone in spite of an MBA, not because of one."

- Elon Musk
  (Business Magnate, Investor, Inventor, Source.)

"For every full-time engineer, add $500,000 in company value. For every full-time MBA, subtract $250,000."

- Guy Kawasaki
  (Venture Capitalist, Entrepreneur & Author.)

"I think an MBA is a complete waste of money. If you have a hole in your knowledge base, there is a ton of online courses you can take. I don't give any advantage to someone in hiring because they have an MBA."

- Mark Cuban
  (Entrepreneur & Investor.)
  https://www.entrepreneur.com/
  article/225357?source=post_page

"Never ever hire an MBA, they will ruin your company."

- Peter Thiel
  (Entrepreneur, Hedge Fund Manager,
  Venture Capitalist and Author.)

"An MBA has become a two-part time machine. First, the students are taught everything they need to know to manage a company from 1990, and second, they are taken out of the real world for two years while the rest of us race as fast as we possibly can."

- Seth Godin
(Author, Entrepreneur, Marketer, and Public Speaker)
https://seths.blog/2005/03/good_news_and_b/

The Road Map

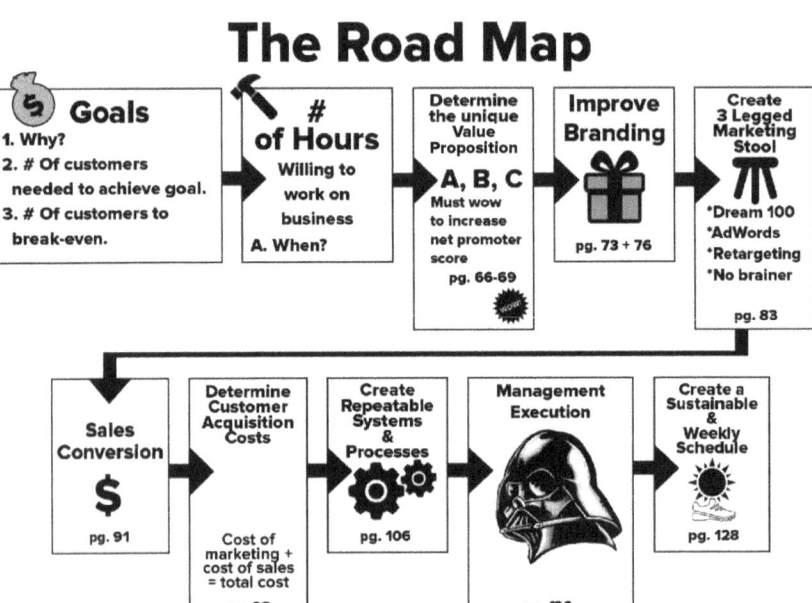

F6 GOALS
1. Faith
2. Family
3. Friendship
4. Fitness
5. Finances
6. Fun

"Rush to Revenue"
Money Cures
All Problems

Regardless of how much formal education you have, the doers and the goal pursuers are the ones that make the most money. Your vast knowledge of the Mesopatamian River Valley and your understanding of Latin isn't going to matter out here in the real world and in the marketplace. In the world of business, you must be able to excel in the areas diagrammed above, or you will lose.

In order to become successful you must realize that nobody is going to wake up tomorrow with a burning desire to pay you, me, or anybody. You must learn to solve problems for real humans on the planet Earth that they are willing to pay you to solve. Then, you must market the heck out of it. For every "yes" you receive, you must first get 100 rejections. That is just how the life of an entrepreneur is.

> ## "BE LIKE A POSTAGE STAMP.
> ## STICK TO IT UNTIL YOU GET THERE."
> ### -HARVEY MACKAY
> ENTREPRENEUR, MOTIVATIONAL SPEAKER AND AUTHOR

DETER MEND
MEDIOCRITY PL.
NOWHERE, UTAH

CLAY CLARK
777 SUCCESS AVE.
74119 TULSA, OK

"NOTABLE QUOTABLES"

"The doers are the major thinkers. The people that really create the things that change this industry are both the doer/thinker in one person."

- Steve Jobs
   (The co-founder of Apple, the former CEO of PIXAR and the founder of NeXT)

"Education is what remains after one has forgotten what one has learned in school."

- Albert Einstein
   (The German-born Jewish theoretical physicist who developed the famous "theory of relativity," which is one of the most important principles of modern physics. He

won the Nobel Prize in Physics in 1921. After successfully fleeing Nazi Germany to save he and his family's life, Albert Einstein alerted President Franklin Delano Roosevelt of the impending danger posed by the atomic bomb being developed by the Nazis. After much push back from President Roosevelt, it was Albert Einstein who finally convinced the President to create the "Manhattan Project" and to invest heavily into the creation of an atomic weapon before the Germans could develop their own atomic bomb. If it were not for the intelligence and the persistence of Albert Einstein the Germans would have fulfilled their plan, and would have successfully dropped an atomic bomb on United States soil. Albert Einstein is one of the key reasons that the Nazi's lost World War II and that people of Jewish faith and ancestry were not completely wiped off the face of the Earth. Before the United States dropped and detonated two nuclear weapons over the Japanese cities of Hiroshima and Nagasaki on August 6 and 9, 1945, respectively, the Nazi's had killed six million Jewish people. Although the two atomic bombings killed between 129,000 and 226,000 people, most of whom were civilians, Albert's sense of urgency and persistence to push President Roosevelt to create a nuclear bomb saved the free world and is responsible for ending World War II.)

Albert Einstein
Old Grove Rd.
Nassau Point
Peconic, Long Island

August 2nd, 1939

F.D. Roosevelt,
President of the United States,
White House
Washington, D.C.

Sir:

Some recent work by E.Fermi and L. Szilard, which has been communicated to me in manuscript, leads me to expect that the element uranium may be turned into a new and important source of energy in the immediate future. Certain aspects of the situation which has arisen seem to call for watchfulness and, if necessary, quick action on the part of the Administration. I believe therefore that it is my duty to bring to your attention the following facts and recommendations:

In the course of the last four months it has been made probable - through the work of Joliot in France as well as Fermi and Szilard in America - that it may become possible to set up a nuclear chain reaction in a large mass of uranium,by which vast amounts of power and large quantities of new radium-like elements would be generated. Now it appears almost certain that this could be achieved in the immediate future.

This new phenomenon would also lead to the construction of bombs, and it is conceivable - though much less certain - that extremely powerful bombs of a new type may thus be constructed. A single bomb of this type, carried by boat and exploded in a port, might very well destroy the whole port together with some of the surrounding territory. However, such bombs might very well prove to be too heavy for transportation by air.

CHAPTER 16

Marketing is Simply a Contest for Getting the
Attention of Your Ideal and Likely Buyers!

"IN A CROWDED MARKETPLACE, FITTING IN IS FAILING. IN A BUSY MARKETPLACE, NOT STANDING OUT IS THE SAME AS BEING INVISIBLE."
– SETH GODIN
(THE *NEW YORK TIMES* BEST-SELLING AUTHOR WHO SOLD HIS COMPANY *YOYODYNE* FOR $30 MILLION.)

Don't allow the concept of marketing your business to become some weird, theoretical, emotion-based, and vague concept. At the end of the day, marketing is simply about gaining the attention of your ideal and likely buyers in this world of perpetual digital distraction and mass-marketing. You must get the attention of your ideal and likely buyers, and when you do finally get their attention, you must get your ideal and likely buyers to take action.

The reason why I had the opportunity to interview Wolfgang Puck is not because I was lucky, because of some spiritual break-through or because "the stars aligned." I was able to interview Wolfgang Puck on *The Thrivetime Show Podcast* because Jonathan Kelly and I have made a list of 4,000 + A-list business success stories that we have wanted to interview on *The Thrivetime Show Podcast,* and if you persistently ask enough people for an opportunity and you have high quality branding representing you, you are eventually going to get a "yes." For my upcoming book, *Mastermind Manuscripts*, I have relentlessly reached out to past guests to ask them for their permission to be included in the upcoming book. I have been told "no" by the best-selling author Seth Godin, the Grammy Award-Winning singer and song-writer, Ross Golan and countless big-time celebrities. However, I have also been told "yes"

by John Maxwell, David Novak, Daniel Pink and 40+ big-time names that you would know. What does this mean to you? How does this relate to you? Stop spiritualizing every rejection and every yes and get busy taking massive action. You have to get yourself to the point mentally where you accept that some will say "yes" and some will say "no," but who cares? Just move on. You have to get yourself emotionally to a place where rejection no longer bothers you at all. I repeat, you must coach yourself up to a place where rejections don't bother you at all. In fact, I've now actually coached myself to a place where I like rejection, I need rejection and I am fueled by rejection.

CHAPTER 17

Design Your Schedule and Design Your Life or
Someone Else Will!

"CONTROL YOUR OWN DESTINY OR SOMEONE ELSE WILL."
– JACK WELCH
(The former CEO of General Electric who grew the company by 4,000% during his tenure.)

As I am writing this book, I am listening to the *Rudy* soundtrack, which is being played via a pair of incredible Yamaha speakers and a Yamaha subwoofer, located underneath my table / desk. As I am writing this book for you, I am 100% focused and I am not distracted. I haven't looked at my phone since Friday, and it is now Sunday. I have not checked my emails and I am 100% locked in. Why? Because I designed my life to be this way. Just a few minutes ago I needed to get up and do a quick stretch break. When I went outside, my view was of a beautiful pool and actual grotto / cave, which we built into our backyard, with a beautiful waterfall that we had built by PoolCreationsInc.com.

Thus far, today, I have interacted with zero negative people. I woke up at 3 AM to begin working on this book. At 6 AM, I was joined by the founder of www.TulsaFitnessSystems.com, Clint Howard, a great member of our team, Jason Beasley, and the founder of www. CompleteCarpetTulsa.com, Nathan Sevrinus, to record a Thrivetime Show podcast episode about persistence.

"ONLY WORK VIA APPOINTMENT."
- CLAY CLARK
(America's #1 Business Coach)

At 8 AM, I was joined by the leadership expert and 9-year client of mine, Clay Staires, to record a podcast to be released on the $100 MBA podcast with Omar Zenhom.

Then, at 10:00 AM, I went upstairs and watched a Life.Church sermon with my family which was being taught by Pastor Craig Groeschel. Why? My day looks like this because I designed it to be this way. However, if I was not intentional, my day would look very different.

If you want to become successful during the short amount of time that we all get to enjoy on the planet Earth, you must learn how to design your days. You must be intentional about your schedule or you will find yourself with a calendar that is loaded up with obligations, and lame conversations with people who are geographically convenient for you to talk to. Design everyday as though it is your last and live like you are dying if you want to live a life worth living.

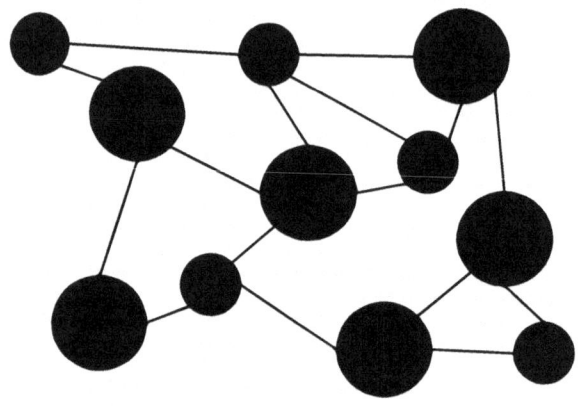

CHAPTER 18

Your Network is Your Net Worth - Stop Hanging Around Negative, Soul-Sucking, Excuse-Making, and Leeching Family, Friends, Employees and Business People!

"ONLY ENGAGE IN MUTUALLY BENEFICIAL
RELATIONSHIPS."
– CLAY CLARK

(Forbes contributing writer. former U.S. Small
Business Administration Entrepreneur of the year
for the state of Oklahoma and the man writing
this book.)

You simply will not reach your highest and best use if you are being held down by the massive ankle weights called your relationships. No matter how motivated you are, if you live in a home where your mother is a gambling addict, your father is a drug addict, or your best friend is always suffering through some urgent, life drama, you simply will not be able to break-free out of this cycle. In order for you to achieve massive success, you must embrace the reality that your network is your net worth and that you will become the average of the 5 people with which you spend the most time.

What drama causing acquaintances, employees, business associates, vendors, family and friends do you need to remove from your life?

Name: _____

Name: _____

Name: _____

Name: _____

Name: _____

Name: _____

Name: _____

Name: _____

CHAPTER 19

You Must Learn to Lead People, to Fire Idiots and
to Become an Enemy of Average or You Will Lose!

"Beware of a herd of people passionately going the wrong direction. This herd mentality is what made Hitler's Nazi party possible."

- Clay Clark

Over the years, I have had the incredible opportunity to help coach, train, and grow many of my previously technician-focused clients into business owning clients who now have both the tenacity and capacity needed to become the leader-developing leaders that every company desperately needs to scale a business. Whether it seems fair or not, your company can simply not grow beyond your capacity to lead your team as their boss.

However, if you are employing a bunch of dumb, distracted, and dishonest idiot employees, nothing is ever going to work, regardless of how solid your leadership skills are. Thus, if you find yourself as the fine employer of a bunch of idiots, it is up to you to diligently and tenaciously set the standard and to fire the morons who are milling around and mucking up the money-making activities that you and your crew must do to make a sustainable profit by solving the problems of your ideal and likely buyers.

"THE LOWER AN INDIVIDUAL'S ABILITY TO LEAD, THE LOWER
THE LID ON HIS POTENTIAL."
- JOHN MAXWELL
(THE NEW YORK TIMES BEST-SELLING
AUTHOR WHO HAS SOLD OVER 20
MILLION BOOKS THROUGHOUT HIS
LIFETIME)

As a leader, you must learn how to work both IN and ON your business. To take your company to the next level, you must learn how to create and document the scalable processes and systems that your company must have in place to go and grow to the next level.

"NOTABLE QUOTABLES"

"There is only one boss. The customer. And he can fire everybody in the company from the chairman on down, simply by spending his money somewhere else."

- Sam Walton
  (The iconic leader behind the founding of Wal-Mart and Sam's Club.)

If you want to take your business to the next level, you must become obsessed with wowing each and every customer that you ever allow to pay you. You must quickly learn that good is the enemy of great in the world of commerce. Thus, you must obsess about creating systems and processes that will wow your ideal and likely buyers every time.

HONEY BADGER ENTREPRENEURS
AN AMERICAN TRADITION
SINCE 1776

As you systematize your business, you must have the tenacity of a honey badger. You see, a honey badger survives as a result of eating snakes and bee larva. A honey badger is constantly getting bitten by snakes and stung by bees and thus, in order to survive, nature has allowed the honey badger to develop an immunity to the venom it receives from snake bites and bee stings. Thus, the honey badger is now nearly immune to the adversity that it is inevitably going to face on a daily basis.

You too must develop this honey badger level of tenacity. You must become the QuikTrip of the convenience store industry, the Chick-fil-A of the fast food industry, and the Apple of the computing and technology industry. You need to embrace the fact that YOU MUST BECOME AN ENEMY OF AVERAGE in order to achieve a massive level of success. You must learn to hate the mediocrity and the attitude of doing "just enough," that is limiting your growth.

CHAPTER 20

Schedule Time for What Matters Most
and Live Intentionally!

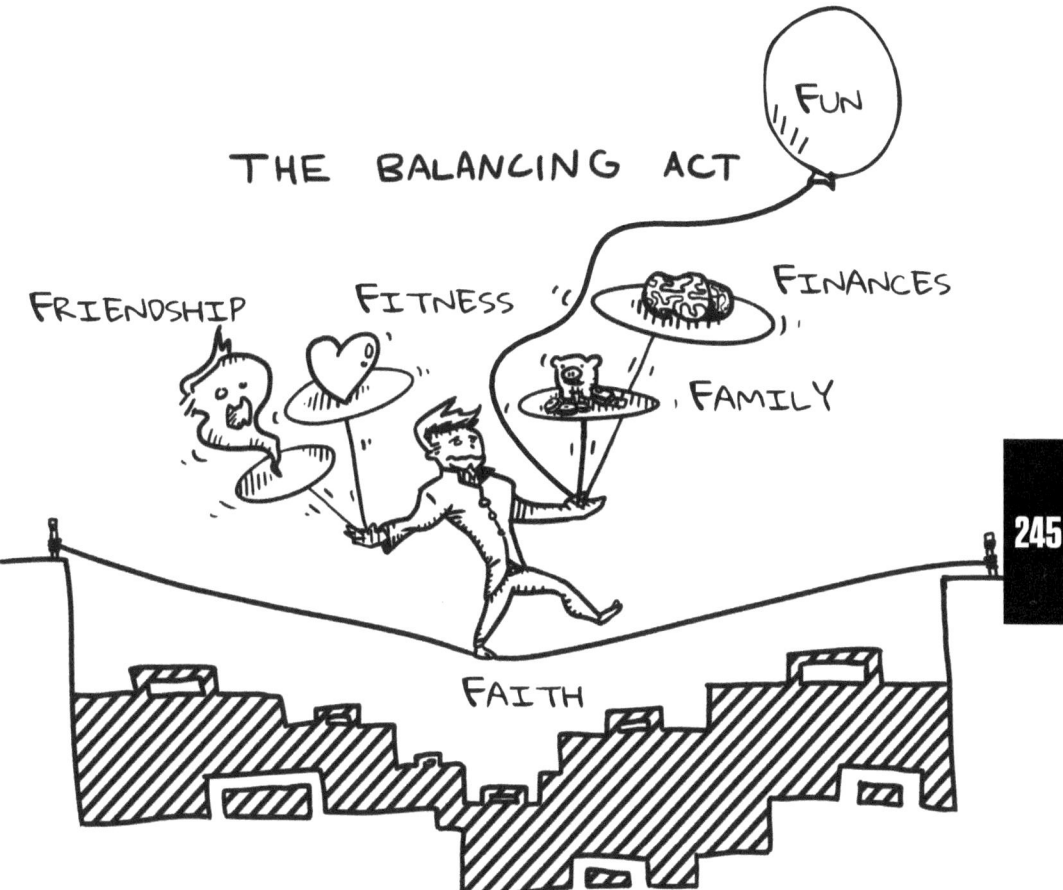

THE BALANCING ACT

FUN

FRIENDSHIP FITNESS FINANCES

FAMILY

FAITH

As your business begins to thrive and as you begin to gain traction in this world of endless distractions, you will quickly discover that there is always "one more thing to do" as it relates to your business. The business that you created will eventually turn into an endless time consuming black hole if you are not intentional about setting time boundaries for the hours that you will allow yourself to work **ON** and **IN** the business.

As a business owner, you will soon discover that there is always one more checklist that needs to be updated, one more script that

DISTRACTION   TRACTION

needs to be improved, and one more system that needs to be enhanced. You will find that there is always "one more hot deal that needs to be closed." However, you do not have an endless amount of time on this planet. Thus, you must become very intentional about designing your days and setting boundaries for the hours that you will allow yourself to work and to devour business related issues and projects. What schedule are you going to choose for your business?

THE LIFE-SUCKING BLACKHOLE KNOWN AS "YOUR BUSINESS!"

"NOTABLE QUOTABLES"

"We need to re-create boundaries. When you carry a digital gadget that creates a virtual link to the office, you need to create a virtual boundary that didn't exist before."

- Daniel Goleman
(The New York Time best-selling author of *Emotional Intelligence*, a former Thrivetime Show guest and one of the world's leading expert on practical modern psychology and emotional intelligence)

When you become very intentional about how you spend your time and whom you spend your time with, you will quickly find yourself enjoying the increased quality of each and every day. When you expect more than others think is possible and you actually take time each morning to block out time for what matters most in your schedule, your quality of life will improve dramatically. Instead of spending your afternoons mindlessly searching around on TV for something to watch, spending your weekend nights at local clubs searching for something to do, and looking in your refrigerator for something random to eat, you will soon find yourself on track and on the task of achieving your goals in all areas of your life. The world has a habit of making room for the person who knows where they are going. Typically, those that go to college go there because they have no idea where they want to end up. Be intentional with your time including only going to college if it is absolutely necessary. Here are some examples of people who knew where they were going and didn't need a college degree to get them there.

"EXPECT MORE THAN OTHERS THINK POSSIBLE."
- HOWARD SCHULTZ

(THE FORMER CHAIR MAN AND CHIEF OF
EXECUTIVE OFFICER OF STARBUCKS.)

Despite not having a college degree, these people went on to victory:

Abraham Lincoln

Despite not having earned the respect of his peers by obtaining a college degree, he went on to become a lawyer and president of the United States. Because he chose to be self-taught, he never did stop learning until the day of his death.

1832 - Lost job and was defeated for state legislature.
1833 - Failed in business.
1843 - Lost his attempt to be nominated for Congress.
1848 - Lost renomination for Congress.
1849 - Rejected in his attempt to become land officer.
1854 - Defeated for U.S. Senate.

Amadeo Peter Giannini

Despite not knowing what he was doing because he didn't have a master's degree from a fancy business college, he went on to become the multi-millionaire founder of Bank of America after dropping out of high school.

Andrew Carnegie

Despite being an elementary school dropout, this man went on to become the world's wealthiest man during his lifetime. Amazing, since he couldn't possibly have known what he was doing because he didn't have a college degree.

Andrew Jackson

This guy went on to become an attorney, a U.S. president, a general, a judge, and a congressman despite being home-schooled and having no formal education at all.

Anne Beiler

The "Princess of Pretzels" went on to start Auntie Anne's Pretzels and to become a millionaire, despite having dropped out of high school. I bet she's disappointed she missed out on the once-in-a-lifetime experiences that so many college graduates with $100,000 of debt enjoyed.

Ansel Adams

I don't know if you are into world-famous photographers or not, but if you are, you know that Ansel Adams became arguably the best photographer in the world despite not graduating from a college of liberal arts. I wonder how he even knew to take the lens cap off of his camera without a college degree.

Barry Diller

This dude may be a billionaire and Hollywood mogul who founded Fox Broadcasting Company, but I am not impressed with him because he does not have a college degree.

Benjamin Franklin

This guy might have invented the Franklin stove, lightning rods, bifocals, and other assorted inventions while working as a founding father of the United States, but I can tell you that he had a hole in his soul where his degree should have been.

Billy Joe (Red) McCombs

Red became a billionaire, but did he have a degree? No. And that is exactly why he doesn't get invited to any of those fancy alumni gatherings, which he would be too busy to attend anyway because he's off counting his money. Seriously, if he started counting the billions of dollars he made by founding Clear Channel media, he would never finish.

Coco Chanel

She may have a perfume that bears her name, but I am not impressed with her because she doesn't have a degree.

Colonel Harlan Sanders

This guy dropped out of elementary school and all he knew about was chicken. Sure he made millions, but I didn't truly have respect for him until he finally earned that law degree by correspondence.

Dave Thomas

Every time I pull into Wendy's to enjoy a delicious snack wrap, I find myself thinking about what a complete waste of talent Dave was. He could have had trillions of dollars if only he had earned a degree.

David Geffen

Like a true loser, he dropped out of college after completing only one year. My, his parents must be disappointed. I feel bad just writing about this billionaire founder of Geffen Records and co-founder of DreamWorks.

David Green

David, oh David. I bet you feel bad about your billions and spend everyday living in regret because you do not have a college degree. I know that you took $600 and famously turned that into billions as the founder of Hobby Lobby, but you could have been a good attorney or a bureaucrat or a politician we all could watch argue to an empty room on C-SPAN.

David Karp

This guy's last name should be carp, because this bottom feeder obviously will never amount to anything — well, except being the multi-millionaire founder of Tumblr. If he hadn't dropped out of school at age 15, I would respect him more.

David Neeleman

This guy started a little airline (JetBlue) to compensate for his lack of a degree. I don't even feel safe on the world's most profitable airline because its founder doesn't have a degree.

David Oreck

David Oreck truly had a career that sucked. This college dropout and multi-millionaire founder of the Oreck vacuum company created vacuums that have sucked the dirt out of carpets for years.

Debbi Fields

Oh, so sad. Little Debbie, the founder of Mrs. Fields Chocolate Chippery, never knew the pride that one could feel upon earning a college degree.

DeWitt Wallace

DeWitt may have founded Reader's Digest, but I'm sure that he could not truly enjoy reading in an intelligent way because he never earned his college degree.

Dustin Moskovitz

Dustin is credited as being one of the founders of that little company called Facebook that only moms, dads, cousins, kids, adults, and humans use. I bet he wishes he had stayed in school at Harvard.

Frank Lloyd Wright

Frank may have become the most famous architect of all time, but I cannot respect a man who never attended high school.

Frederick Henry Royce

Okay, so a Rolls-Royce is a symbol of automotive excellence for many people, but this guy had to have been compensating for the fact that he knew nothing about anything because he was an elementary school dropout.

George Eastman

Perhaps you are not old enough to know about the Kodak brand that used to control the world as part of the Illuminati. How George founded this little company despite dropping out of high school is beyond me. It's so sad.

H. Wayne Huizenga

Wayne is a beautiful man and founder of WMX Garbage Company, and he also helped launch the Blockbuster Video chain. Good for him! Because without a degree, he was basically screwed.

Henry Ford

Okay, so I've mentioned this guy in the book, but without a college degree, you can bet this billionaire founder of the Ford Motor Company was never respected by his father-in-law.

Henry J. Kaiser

This multimillionaire and founder of Kaiser Aluminum didn't even graduate from high school. Think about it. Without a diploma, there was no way he could have become one of those pharmaceutical reps who delivers sales presentations and catering to doctors every day in exchange for their allegiance in writing prescriptions for the drugs the rep is peddling.

Hyman Golden

This guy spent his whole life making drinks and millions. I bet you the founder of Snapple lived a life of regret while endlessly chanting to himself, "Why me? No Degree. Why me? No degree."

Ingvar Kamprad

I believe IKEA's business model is in jeopardy. Their founder has no degree. The lines of customers are now so long that no one even wants to go there anymore. Oh...and he's dyslexic.

Isaac Merrit Singer

This sewing machine inventor dropped out of high school because he was spending all his time sewing. I am SEW sorry for him.

Jack Crawford Taylor

Although this man did serve honorably as a World War II fighter pilot for the Navy, I wonder what he is going to fall back on if his Enterprise Rent-a-Car venture fails.

James Cameron

Avatar...overrated. Titanic...overrated. Winning an Oscar... overrated. But what did you expect from a director, writer, and film guy who dropped out of college?

Jay Van Andel

A billionaire co-founder of Amway...not impressive without a degree. He does not know the meaning of life.

Jerry Yang

Who even uses Yahoo anyway, other than the 20% of the world that does? This guy threw it all away and dropped out of a PhD program. I bet you he can't even spell "Yahoo!"

Jimmy Dean

Food is so simple. You grow it. You eat it. You raise it. You kill it and eat it. How complex could it be if a man was able to start this multi-million dollar company after dropping out of high school at age 16?

Jimmy Iovine

This man grew up as the son of a secretary and a longshoreman. However, at the age of 19 his ambition had become his mission. Obsessed with making records, he began working as a studio professional around the year of 1972 when a friend of his got him a job cleaning a recording studio. Soon he found himself recording with John Lennon, Bruce Springsteen and other top artists. In 1973 he landed a full-time job on the staff of the New York recording studio, Record Plant where he worked on Meat Loaf's *Bat Out of Hell* album and Springsteen's *Born to Run* album. He went on to be involved in the production of more than 250 million albums. In 2006, Iovine teamed with Dr. Dre to found Beats Electronics. This company was purchased by Apple for $3 billion in May 2014. I hope he goes on to be successful despite not having a degree.

John D. Rockefeller Sr.

So my son and I did name our Great Pyrenees dog after this man, but we wouldn't have named a human after him, because although Rockefeller became the wealthiest man in the world, he didn't have a degree and I judge him for this.

John Mackey

The guy who founded Whole Foods Market, the millennial mecca of the great organic panic that has swept our nation, enrolled and dropped out of college six times. Now he's stuck working at a grocery store in a dead-end job.

John Paul DeJoria

This man is the billionaire co-founder of John Paul Mitchell Systems and dude who also founded Patron Spirits. That's it. That's all he's accomplished. No degree.

Joyce C. Hall

This guy spent his whole life writing apology cards to his family for shaming him for not graduating from college. When he wasn't doing that, he was running that little company he founded called Hallmark.

Kemmons Wilson

This dude started the Holiday Inn chain after dropping out of high school. But then what? What's he doing now? Well he's not buying huge amounts of college logo apparel and running down to the college football stadium eight Saturdays per year while talking about the good old days with his frat brothers because he doesn't have a degree.

Kevin Rose

This dude dropped out of college and started a company called Digg.com. I'm not impressed with his millions. I just want to see that degree.

Kirk Kerkorian

I did see a Boyz II Men concert at the Mirage Resorts that this guy owns. But, I have never stayed at the Mandalay Bay resort that he owns in Las Vegas more than once. It's good that he owns MGM Studios because the closest he'll ever come to a degree is if he makes a movie about himself getting a degree. He dropped out of school in 8th grade.

Larry Ellison

Larry is the billionaire co-founder of Oracle software company and he is a man who dropped out of two different colleges. Oh, the regret he must feel.

Leandro Rizzuto

This guy spent his time building Conair and that was it. Now, just because he is a billionaire, does he think we should respect him even though he does not have a degree?

Leslie Wexner

My wife buys stuff from the L Brands (the global retail empire that owns Victoria's Secret, Bath & Body Works, and Limited), but I am still not impressed with the fact that this law school dropout started a billion-dollar brand with $5,000.

Mark Ecko

If you are one of those people who has success based upon the success you have, then I suppose Mark Ecko is impressive. This multi-millionaire is the founder of Mark Ecko Enterprises, but he dropped out of college.

Mary Kay Ash

I feel like Prince should have written a song about the pink Cadillacs that Mary Kay was famous for giving to her top sales reps. But I am not impressed with her because she didn't attend college.

Michael Dell

He may be the billionaire founder of Dell Computers, but he probably doesn't feel like a billionaire since he never experienced the college joys of drunken music festivals and regrettable one-night stands.

Milton Hershey

Like I always say, "If you drop out of 4th grade you are going to spend your entire life making chocolate." That is what the founder of Hershey's Milk Chocolate did.

Rachael Ray

Her happiness and genuine love for people and food makes me mad because without formal culinary arts training, this Food Network cooking show star and food industry entrepreneur is just a sham.

Ray Kroc

He dropped out of high school, founded McDonald's, and spent his whole life saying, "Do you want fries with that?" So sad.

Richard Branson

So he's the billionaire founder of Virgin Records, Virgin Atlantic Airways, Virgin Mobile, and more. But did he graduate from high school? No. He dropped out of his high school at the age of 16. So sad.

Richard Schulze

He's the Best Buy founder, but he did not attend college. Doesn't he know that the investment in a college degree is truly the Best Buy you can ever make?

Rob Kalin

Rob is the founder of Etsy, but who even uses Etsy other than all of the humans on earth? This dude flunked out of high school, then he enrolled in art school. He created a fake student ID for MIT so he could take the courses that he wanted. His professors were so impressed by his scam that they actually helped him get into NYU. Rob, you have to get it together.

Ron Popeil

The dude who is constantly talking about dehydrating your meat and the multimillionaire founder of Ronco did not graduate from college.

Rush Limbaugh

This guy irritates half of America every day for three hours per day. I believe that this multi-millionaire media maven and radio talk show host would be more liked if he had graduated from a liberal arts college and would have purchased a Prius preloaded with left-wing bumper stickers.

Russell Simmons

This guy is co-founder of Def Jam records and the founder of the Russell Simmons Music Group. He's also the founder of Phat Farm fashions and a bestselling author. He didn't graduate from college because he claims to have been too busy introducing rap and hip hop music to the planet.

S. Daniel Abraham

This man founded Slim-Fast without even having a degree in nutrition. Outside of the millions of people who use his products every day to lose weight, who is going to trust him with their health since he doesn't even have a college degree?

Sean John Combs

The man who is en route to becoming the first hip-hop billionaire in part because of his ownership in the Ciroc Vodka brand did not graduate from college because he was spending his time discovering and promoting Mary J. Blige, The Notorious B.I.G., Jodeci, and other R&B stars. If this man ever wants to become truly successful, he will go back to Howard University and get that degree.

Shawn Fanning

This is the music industry-killing devil who created Napster and went on to become a multi-millionaire. If he would have stayed in college, he would have learned to follow the rules.

Simon Cowell

This famous TV producer, judger of people, American Idol, The X Factor, and Britain's Got Talent star dropped out of high school. He has been negative ever since. He obviously needs a college degree to calm him down because I've never met a college graduate who is mean.

Steve Jobs

This hippie dropped out of college and frankly, his little Apple company barely made it.

Steve Madden

Steve dropped out of college and now spends his entire life making shoes. He may be worth millions, but I'm sure that you and I are not impressed.

Steve Wozniak

Okay, so I did know that Steve Jobs co-founded Apple with this guy and both of them became billionaires, but they experienced what I call a "hollow success" because they did not take the time to earn a college degree.

Theodore Waitt

This man became a billionaire by selling a PC to every human possible during the 1990s. He may have co-founded Gateway computers but without a degree, how will he ever experience true success? I bet that he regrets not having a degree.

Thomas Edison

Tommy Boy wasn't smart enough to graduate from high school, yet he was crazy enough to invent the modern light bulb, recorded audio, and recorded video. I am never impressed with crazy people who don't graduate from high school.

Tom Anderson

This dude co-founded MySpace after dropping out of high school. He made his millions, but who ever had a MySpace account anyway?

Ty Warner

I think the only thing weirder than collecting Beanie Babies is to have invented them. To cover up this weird Beanie Babies fixation, this billionaire has gone on to purchase real estate. College would have taught him that it is not normal for an adult to be interested in stuffed animals.

Vidal Sassoon

This dude founded Vidal Sassoon after dropping out of high school. Had he graduated from college, I'm sure his product would have been better.

W. Clement Stone

This guy started the billion-dollar insurance company called Combined Insurance. He then went on to start *Success* Magazine and write books to keep himself busy because he felt so bad that he didn't have a college degree.

Wally "Famous" Amos

This man did not graduate from high school and spent almost his entire working career making people fat by selling them Famous Amos cookies. If he had graduated from college, he might have invented a product that makes people thin and able to live forever while tasting good, you know, like carrots.

Walt Disney

This struggling entrepreneur who never really figured it out co-founded the Walt Disney Company with his brother Roy. He didn't even graduate from high school, which is probably why he spent his entire life drawing cartoons.

Wolfgang Puck

Okay, so my wife and I buy his soup. Okay, so I have eaten at his restaurant a few times. But I can't respect a man who dropped out of high school at the age of 14. Yes, he's opened up 16 restaurants and 80 bistros. So what? Respecting people like this sets a bad example for kids because not everyone can go on to become a successful entrepreneur, but everyone can incur $100,000 of student loan debt before finding a soul-sucking job doing something they don't like in exchange for a paycheck.

WANT TO LEARN MORE SO THAT YOU CAN EARN MORE?

THROUGHOUT THE YEARS CLAY HAS WRITTEN THE FOLLOWING BOOKS.

START HERE

The World's Best Business Growth & Consulting Book: Business Growth Strategies from the World's Best Business Coach.

F6 JOURNAL

Meta Thrive Time Journal.

WHEEL OF WEALTH

An Entrepreneur's Action Guide.

JACKASSARY

Jackassery will serve as a beacon of light for other entrepreneurs that are looking to avoid troublesome employees and difficult situations. This is real. This is raw. This is unfiltered entrepreneurship.

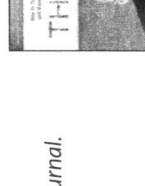

THRIVE

How to Take Control of Your Destiny and Move Beyond Surviving... Now!

NOT LONELY AT THE TOP

15 Keys to Achieving a successful, peaceful, and drama free life.

DON'T LET YOUR EMPLOYEES HOLD YOU HOSTAGE

This candid book shares how to avoid being held hostage by employees.

THE ART OF GETTING THINGS DONE

Clay Clark breaks down the proven, time-tested and time freedom creating super moves that you can use to create both the time freedom and financial freedom that most people only dream about.

THE ENTREPRENEUR'S DRAGON ENERGY

The Mindset Kanye, Trump and You Need to Succeed.

WILL NOT WORK FOR FOOD

9 Big Ideas for Effectively Managing Your Business in an Increasingly Dumb, Distracted & Dishonest America.

MAKE YOUR LIFE EPIC

Clay shares his journey and struggle from the dorm room to the board room during his raw and action-packed story of how he built DJConnection.com.

SEARCH ENGINE DOMINATION

The proven plan, best practice processes - super moves to make million with online marketing.

BOOM

The 13 Proven Steps to Business Success.

PODCAST DOMINATION

The process and path to podcast success.

MAKE THE WORLD A BETTER PLACE

Subscribe to the ThriveTime Show Podcast today at www.ThriveTimeShow.com